AF244027

WRITE HERE, WRITE NOW
VOLUME 1

REAL WRITERS NEVER QUIT

What hundreds of authors reveal
about not giving up

WAYNE KELLY

2026 edition published in the UK by Pick Lock Publishing
ISBN: 978-1-9195361-0-1

Copyright © 2026 by Wayne Kelly
All rights reserved.

Wayne Kelly has asserted his right under the Copyright, Designs and Patents Act
1988 to be identified as the author of this work.

No part of this book may be reproduced in any form or by any electronic or me-
chanical means, including information storage and retrieval systems, without written permission from the publisher, except for the use of brief quotations in a review.

This book is a work of non-fiction and reflects the author's personal experience and
opinion. Excerpts from The Write Place Podcast are reproduced from interviews
with the respective authors.

Cover design and typesetting by Wayne Kelly for WKW Productions
www.wkwproductions.co.uk

*For anyone who has sat before a blank sheet
of paper or stared at that hungry, blinking cursor…*

I salute you. You're one of us.

A Note on Quotes

The voices in this book come from hundreds of conversations recorded over many years on *The Write Place* podcast and *The Joined Up Writing Podcast*. To make those spoken words work in print, some quotes have been edited for flow and brevity. Where edits have been made, I've stayed as close as possible to the original meaning and tone.

These words remain the speakers' own, shaped only enough to be clear and readable on the page.

Contents

Introduction

Emily Houghton, Episode 148

Why should you read this book? I've published two novels, but I'm not a famous best-selling author with millions of sales behind me. I've written and directed short films and produced documentaries, but I doubt you've ever seen many, or any, of them. That said, I've been passionate about words from the moment I learned to read and I've been writing stories since I could hold a pen.

The desire to create characters and worlds and to pour my heart out onto the page, drives everything I do – even if I haven't always been able to make a living from it. I'm a normal person, just like you, who has learned my craft on the job, writing multiple novels – some published, some not. Through critique, through rejection, through trial and error. Across multiple mediums, from short stories to scripts and novels, I've done it all and more for almost the entirety of my time on this planet. The point is, wherever you are in your writing journey right now… I've been there too*[1]. Suffering from self-doubt and imposter syndrome? I feel your pain. Stuck in the middle of a first draft? Can't see a way out? I've been lost far too many times to count. There's no getting around it: Writing is hard. It took me decades to publish my first book. How did I make it at all?

Because I didn't quit, and by the time you've finished this book, neither will you.

For me, the real revelation came when I realised EVERY writer goes through all of these stages and plenty more besides – even those incredibly successful multi-award-winning ones. I came to this realisation after spending more than a decade interviewing hundreds of authors for *The Write Place* podcast. From debut authors to bestsellers and everyone in between, I've asked about their path to publication, their struggles, their highs and lows. They've given me their tips and talked about their process. Each has a different story to tell and a unique perspective, and yet the same themes and strands run through almost all of my interviews. Most writers and creatives are plagued with feelings of inadequacy, worrying they don't belong or that they're not a 'real writer'. Even writers who've published dozens of books have told me they're convinced they won't be able to do it again.

"What hasn't changed is the self-doubt, you know, chronic self-doubt."

Joanna Penn, Episode 65

---

[1] Unless you've sold millions of books and are living in luxury in some idyllic paradise.

Aside from finding all those conversations so fascinating, these recurring themes and concerns have given me some kind of perverse comfort. Maybe I'm not so strange after all. Perhaps I do belong here. If Joanna Penn, New York Times bestselling author of dozens of books is telling me she still wonders whether she can continue to be successful, then surely there's hope for mere mortals like us? All of these accomplished, critically and commercially successful people were once like you, scratching out writing hours between busy work and family lives, and finding a way to finish their books. Many of them still are. *The Write Place*, and the friends and relationships I've gained from it, have given me the courage to pursue my own writing aspirations. I may not currently be bothering the Sunday Times bestseller list or be in line for a Booker Prize, but I've published two novels, with another on the way. I've written several award-winning short films and produced a feature-length documentary. I'm convinced a lot of that achievement was fuelled by the confidence and knowledge I've gained from *The Write Place*. After hundreds of hours quizzing people who've made their writing aspirations a reality, it's been a well of information and inspiration to me, and hopefully to many of my listeners. And now, with this book, I hope to bring even more of you into the fold and share some of that wisdom and insight.

Chapter by chapter, I'll lead you through my own writing journey, illustrated with quotes and snippets of knowledge and inspiration from some of my amazing *The Write Place* guests. I believe my story will resonate with many of you – precisely because it isn't some epic journey full of high drama. My writing life probably mirrors many of yours. I'm just a working-class bloke who always dreamed of being a writer but had no idea how to get there. A man who spent years doing jobs he hated, to support a young family. Struggling to find the time to be creative and feeling like I'd never make it. Someone who had no idea of where I was going yet was compelled to keep pushing forward anyway. There have been so many times when I was ready to give up.

I'll tell you how I turned things around and why I believe I'm a stronger person and a better writer because of it. I'll show you why you don't need to be extraordinary to be a writer. You just need the will to persevere in the face of constant doubt, rejection and life's obstacles. I'll tell you how I did that, and how many of my guests pulled it off too. We'll end each chapter with practical advice and exercises to help you at every stage of your journey.

I'll help you to remember why you fell in love with writing in the first place and show you how to tap into that, whenever you hit a rocky patch. We'll talk about process – *how* you write. We'll tackle self-doubt and find ways to shrug off imposter syndrome. I'll share how I decided to dig an escape tunnel from the job I hated, to get to the creative freedom I craved, and show you how you can do the same. We'll talk about momentum and community and the power of critique. We'll explore rejection and how you can deal with setbacks and hearing the word 'no' over and over again.

Writing has helped me through difficult periods in my life and many of my podcast guests have talked about writing as therapy. I share their tips on how writing can aid mental health and give you exercises to try yourself. I'll tell you about my own journey to publication and why I chose a different path to traditional publishing. All of this is followed by a whole chapter at the end of the book dedicated to powerful quotes from the podcast. A well of inspiration you can dip into anytime you need a boost or are looking for practical help and advice.

I'll give you the tools and the inspiration to start your next novel or story, to finish that first draft and get your book out into the world and into the hands of your readers. I'll help you to see what's already obvious to me, because you picked up this book in the first place:

You are a writer.

And real writers never quit.

So are you ready to build your stamina, get unstuck and get inspired?

Then let's do it together, write here, write now.

1

The Call to Write

Finding your first spark

> "I always knew I wanted to be an author, and I suppose I was just fortunate no one told me that was a ridiculous idea."
>
> Hanna Jameson, Episode 98

During the fallow writing periods, the times when we're struggling to find the inspiration or motivation to get back to the page, it helps to remember how and why we began to write. Or perhaps you're only now about to embark on your writing journey? Take a moment to think about where that desire came from. Though all our origin stories are unique, they often share many of the same elements and creative sparks. Since the podcast began, asking my guests how they came to writing has always been an integral part of the show. Some of them knew they were writers from an early age, and some came to it later on, but all of them eventually fell in love with the written word. In this chapter, I'll share some snippets of their stories and mine, before showing you how to use your origin story to get you through periods of adversity, or set you on the right path from the get-go.

Taxi driver

Before we get into a bit of my backstory, here's a guest anecdote from 2015, that I still remember to this day. It was from Tony Schumacher, a Liverpool-born writer who, at the time of recording, had written two successful alternate history novels. He had previously been a police officer but then found himself doing night shifts as a taxi driver…

"One night I picked up a lady in Liverpool, a passenger, and she got in the back of the cab and we were chatting. I asked her what she did for a living. She told me she edited a magazine. And I just said, 'Oh, I do a bit of writing.'

She said, 'What do you write about?'

I had to think of something quick, so I said, 'I write about what happens in the cab. It's a blog.' She asked me what it was called and, because I was looking at it, I said, 'It's called *In the Rearview Mirror.*'"

At this point, incredulous, I asked Tony why he'd said this. He told me:

"My whole life is built on lies, really! She gave me her card and asked me to email something to her."

Tony then drove to a park and wrote what would become his first piece for a monthly column called '*In the Rearview Mirror*'. He drew on his experiences as a police officer and discovered he had a passion and talent for writing which must have been lying dormant for years. More recently, Tony went one step further and wrote the successful BBC TV series, *Responder*. And it all started with that casual lie in the back of a late-night taxi.

Discovering magic

Unlike Tony, I knew I wanted to write from an early age. Do you remember when you learned to read? I don't mean, the approximate age. I'm talking about the exact moment something clicked in your brain and suddenly this incredible gateway to another world opened and revealed a place you didn't even know existed. I do. Or at least, I think I remember. It's been said that memories are nothing more than the stories we tell ourselves, so maybe this is just the one I created for myself – but then again, I'm a writer, so what did you expect?

Here's how I remember it. I think I was five. There had been a few weeks or months of our teacher writing letters and words on the board, sounding them out and trying to get us to remember what each of these squiggles meant. At some point, we began to work through the usual picture books you're given at that age. On each page was a picture and underneath a short sentence like 'Here is an apple.' We'd be called up one-by-one to sit with our teacher as she pointed at the words and we pretended we could read. At least, to me, it felt like pretending. I wasn't reading at all. I was *remembering*. Of course, Miss Wardale was no idiot. She knew what I was up to. Sometimes she would even ask me outright and I smiled sweetly… and lied through my teeth.

**"Writing just came to me naturally
because I loved books. But it wasn't until
I was eleven or twelve years old, when it
crystallised for me that this is what I wanted
to do and this is what I was born to do."**

Maram Taibah, Episode 127

A few weeks later, I was sitting on a chair at the end of the dining table at my grandma's house, legs dangling, as I looked at another book. I frowned and focused on these weird black shapes grown-ups insisted were *words*. I was looking at the first clump of letters at the beginning of the sentence, my finger pressed to the scratchy dry paper beneath it, when something weird happened. I began to sound out the letters…

"Thhhh… uh. M-a-n. Man. Huh-a-sss. Has. A. Big. Hat."

Huh, I remember thinking, *maybe I'm just cheating again*. Until the penny dropped and I realised I hadn't read this book before. My little five-year-old heart began to beat faster. I read it again, quicker this time. Maybe it was a fluke. I turned the page. I barely glanced at the picture, desperate to see if this magic was a one-off.

"The. Boy. Has. A. Dog."

My tiny mind was blown. It's no exaggeration to say, once I truly grasped the power of words, that the world was a new place for me. I began to read all the time, anything I could find. Crisp packets, cereal boxes, captions on the TV. I would say the words out loud and ask the nearest adult to tell me if I was saying it correctly. Although sometimes my mistake was obvious, like the time Mum and Dad burst out laughing when the motor racing came on. The title card popped up and I blurted out:

"GRAND PRICKS!"

The Grand Prix incident was probably the first time I discovered words didn't always sound the way they looked. Far from finding this frustrating, I was thrilled by it. It quickly became apparent that *words* was my thing. Or should that be words *were* my thing? See, I told you. It's my calling.

Guest Gail Aldwin's writing journey began with a literal journey… to the other side of the world.

"At twenty, I left London and caught a double-decker bus that went to Kathmandu. That was the start of many travels. At that time, you just wrote letters. That was really the start of me enjoying writing."

Gail Aldwin, Episode 143

The urge to write

From the moment I could form some words on a page, I was off and running, desperate to create my own stories. Back then my biggest influence was Roald Dahl. I couldn't get enough of his books. From *The Twits* to *James and the Giant Peach*, to *The BFG* and everything in between, RD was where it was at. He seemed to intuitively understand that as far as children were concerned, no idea or premise was too outlandish. I found his originality thrilling and that's probably the reason I've never been interested in slavishly copying stories I've read before, or writing fan fiction. I know many writers learned their craft that way, but it wasn't for me.

Getting schooled – why teachers matter

Writing was now something I counted as one of my hobbies. I genuinely did it for fun, at weekends, during school holidays or whenever I found myself alone with pen and paper. When I was ten, I wrote a poem for a regional writing competition.

To my surprise, I was shortlisted and was asked to attend the award ceremony, where I had to get up on stage and read out the poem. In front of a room made up of a hundred or so parents and children, I stood as confidently as I could and delivered my piece called 'The Machine Gunners'.

The reading was nerve-racking but thrilling and was my first taste of objective encouragement. It was also the first time I dared to dream of being *A Writer*. Whatever that was.

> **"I remember this one brilliant teacher at primary
> school. She would read us stories, and it would
> be the end of the day and the story wouldn't
> have finished… I always remember she'd say,
> 'Go and write your own ending to the story.'"**
>
> Joanna Wallace, Episode 198

I went off to high school, hoping for more opportunities to write stories and was fortunate enough to be placed in the class of Mr Williams. He regularly found ways to make creative writing part of his teaching. My favourite assignments were always when we were given free rein to come up with our own stories. I loved my English lessons, and it was the first time I had a passionate, encouraging teacher who gave me real, constructive feedback to help me improve. There was one piece of advice Mr Williams gave me back then that I still use today.

"Lead your reader by the hand through this new world you are creating and be sure to use all five senses."

John Williams, English Teacher (retired),
Martin High School.

Sadly, my time at high school with Mr Williams had to come to an end, but before I left, aged fourteen, we had a visit from the careers adviser. It still irks me to this day.

I'm from an ordinary working-class background. My mum worked in a factory and my dad was a window cleaner. Both of them hardworking and intelligent, but neither of them ever in a position to pursue any academic aspirations they had. Despite that – maybe *because* of that – they were always supportive and encouraging of my efforts at school and were keen for me to eventually go to university. From an early age they used to tell anyone who would listen that I was going to be a journalist. Why a journalist? Well, that was the only kind of writer we knew about. Mum and Dad were both big readers – Mum fiction, Dad non-fiction – but we had no inkling of how I might become a novelist. This is decades before the internet, and we didn't know anyone who was even remotely connected with that world. So, the plan, if it could be called that, was to become a journalist, because that was a 'real job' we knew existed. That's as deep as their, or my, knowledge went and it was good enough for me. I had something to aim for. So when I was told I had an appointment with the careers adviser, I was excited to describe my plans and ask for advice.

"Ooh,' said the middle-class woman in a beige cardigan, "that's very hard to get into. Are you sure there isn't anything else you'd like to do?"

What an inspiring speech. It was hardly up there with "O Captain, my Captain!", was it? What I've come to believe since, is she was actually saying something very different.

"That's very hard *for someone like you* to get into…" is what she was inferring.

Or, maybe, you know, I've just got a massive chip on my shoulder, and she didn't mean that at all. Who knows? Either way, she didn't give me any information out of her little box of cards, and I couldn't think of anything else I wanted to do.

> **"This is my passion and what I want to do with my life, and I wasn't going to let one setback take anything away from where I was going."**
>
> Lauren North, Episode 135

Was I really cut out to be a writer?

When I was sixteen, I finally managed to get some work experience at one of the local newspapers. It was dull and dry, but then two things happened that would eventually lead me back to writing again. Firstly, I performed in the upper sixth cabaret. A friend and I took on Monty Python's 'Dead Parrot' sketch. Obviously, I didn't write that, but transcribing it from an old VHS cassette, and seeing how it was put together, made me want to have a go myself. And when the performance itself went well, I also found I'd been 'bitten by the bug' and was desperate to do it again. I put on my own show at college and wrote all the sketches.

Around the same time, I found music and joined a band as the lead singer. Only a couple of months before, I'd been scuttling along corridors, trying to keep out of the way of the big kids and become invisible. Now here I was, fronting a band, with aspirations of being a comedy writer and performer.

I'd be lying if I said I didn't get a kick out of being on stage with the band, but the real high has always been writing and performing my own songs. Despite all that, back then it was still easier to call myself a 'singer in a band' than it was to say, 'I'm a writer'.

The perfect example of my thinking around this time was when I was chatting to a friend, just after we had completed our A levels. She was middle class, really bright and despite attending state school like me, had gained a place at Cambridge or Oxford – I can't remember which. She was asking me what I wanted to do with my life.

"Surely you'll get a job in TV or something?" she said.

"With your writing and everything."

I laughed, honestly thinking she was joking. She frowned and looked genuinely confused at my reaction. We never talked about it again. What she didn't understand was that, coming from my background, the idea of 'getting a job in TV or something' may as well have been asking me if I was going to find peace in the Middle East. This sounds like an excuse, but at the time that's how I felt. People like me didn't become novelists or 'work in TV'. Of course, as I've grown older, I've realised that's not true at all. Some working-class people, like Tony Schumacher, and many of my other guests, do make it through, but in the moment, I didn't believe it was possible. I wish I'd realised back then, right at the beginning, that I wasn't *becoming* a writer. I already was one.

"If I read a book and I didn't like the ending as a child, I would rip that page out and re-write it. It was something that was just in me, I suppose."

Ericka Waller, Episode 151

WRITE HERE, WRITE NOW

1. **Ask yourself, 'Why do I write?'** Rediscover your writing origin story. Write out at least three things you love or loved about writing. What was the initial spark? When did writing feel inevitable?

2. **Make it visible.** Pin your list to the wall. Every time you're losing your way or struggling to find motivation, take a look, reconnect and find your mojo again.

2
What if I'm Not a Real Writer?

Battling self-doubt

> "Even today, I'm sitting there thinking *is this good enough? Can I do this?* I have to really give myself a talking to – *you've done this eight times before and you can do it again.* But the imposter syndrome still creeps in."
>
> AJ Campbell, Episode 215

Self-doubt. It's something almost every writer battles with. It can destroy confidence, motivation and, ultimately, productivity. How many times have you struggled to finish a book, a chapter or even a sentence because you're racked with feelings of inadequacy? I certainly have and, for many years, I naively thought this was something only 'amateur' or 'hobbyist' writers experienced. *The Write Place* showed me that no matter how successful you become, self-doubt never truly goes away.

I've come to realise that instead of trying to climb out of the icy pool of self-doubt, we should be settling in for the long haul. Get acclimatised, because it's an important part of the process. This chapter looks at how you can move past 'learning to live with it' and instead, use it to fuel your work.

Leaving school – what now?

Between the band, writing sketches and all the other distractions, it was obvious my grades were going to suffer.

When I got my A level results, let's just say they were pretty poor. As far as I was concerned, this only gave me two options: full-time work in a job that didn't require a degree or worldwide success as the singer in a band. One of those was more realistic than the other…

I asked for full-time hours at Tesco, the supermarket where I'd been working part-time while at college.

Things began well. The first few months were great. I was freed from the shackles of homework, revision and the dread of failing another exam. I had money in my pocket and two of my friends had taken a year out, which meant we could still meet up a couple of times a week and blow all my wages on beer.

Yet within a few months, I was depressed, not sleeping and losing my temper over the smallest of issues. I felt like I'd blown up my entire life, all because I hadn't performed well in my exams. To cut a very long story short, my parents encouraged me to go back to university. I stayed local but chose a subject that was so far removed from my interests and natural abilities – Multimedia Computing?! – that by the second term, I was out of my depth and bored out of my brains. Whilst all of this had been going on, I'd been performing three or four times a week in a cover band, but now I was sick of that too. Looking back, I can see I was creating a toxic myth about myself: I was someone who never finished anything.

"I think in my mind... writers should be able to step outside of their comfort zone, in the characters they know and the location they know, and be able to write a completely different book, like learning another language."

Karin Salvalaggio, Episode 95

Sometimes, it's the fear of failure that holds us back. Bead Roberts, an experienced writing tutor and long-time writing friend of mine, has always given out straight-talking advice. I interviewed her back in 2017 and asked her what guidance she had for writers who struggle to find the courage to finish and then submit their work for publication or competitions.

> "Nobody is going to come knocking on your
> door asking, 'Do you have anything in a
> drawer?' You don't have to tell anybody.
> Just send something. You're not the only
> one who's failed to be the winner or to be
> shortlisted. There will be hundreds, sometimes
> thousands of other people. And what you
> need to do is buy the anthology, or look at the
> winning story and ask yourself,
> 'Why didn't my story win?' Learn from it."

Bead Roberts, Episode 53

Brought to book

I quit the university course and the band and took the easy option… back to full-time hours at Tesco. This time there would be no more messing around. It was time to get serious, to forget all these silly pie-in-the-sky notions of having a creative career. I got on the management programme and settled down to a career in retail. I sleep-walked through the next few months, wearing a mask of fake enthusiasm for the world of middle management. Everything was going to be just fine…

I think the moment I decided it was time to leave was when a woman burst a bag of frozen peas over my head because I'd told her the store was closing.

While I looked for another job, I began to write what would be my first novel. I was really into Nick Hornby and Mike Gale at the time, so the story was a comic spin on my life at that moment, with an emotional through-line about friendship. I poured out my heart on the page and tried to put a brave face on the fact I was stressed and depressed.

I continued to chip away at the book, but my immediate issue was getting out of the stressful environment of retail. I was working long hours, eating rubbish and drinking too much red wine on my nights off. More than once I woke up with purple lips. Yes, really.

I applied for a job at HSBC Bank to become a management trainee. Was it because I was passionate about a career in retail banking? No. I hated working weekends, and this was Monday to Friday. Life just seemed simpler back then.

Around this time, I finished the book I'd been working on. It was a novella called *To Be Honest*. I had no idea what to do with it. At the time I knew nothing about editing and revision. I thought you simply wrote a novel and then made sure all the spelling and grammar was correct. I knew the book wasn't good enough and was beginning to believe I was foolish for even attempting to write it. What was I thinking? Does this sound familiar to any of you?

"Not everyone who starts a book finishes a book. So if by some miracle I am managing to do this, maybe I should respect that process and stop beating myself up about it."

Sarah Painter, Episode 94

Unfortunately, I saw *To Be Honest* as a waste of time, another example of my ineptitude. In any case, it didn't matter. While I continued to question myself, fate intervened. I discovered I was going to be a dad. I was twenty-three. The time really had come to knuckle down, focus on a 'proper' career and prepare for the arrival of my beautiful daughter, Megan.

Over a decade of talking to other writers – many of them best-selling authors with dozens of books behind them – I came to realise that all creatives suffer bouts of self-doubt. It's part of the deal. It's all in how we frame it. Constantly asking ourselves if we deserve to be called a writer will only result in crippling anxiety. The words dry up and it all seems pointless. It's good to question if our work is good enough, but don't question what you are. If you write… you're a writer.

I printed out the novel and put it in a drawer, for my

eyes only. I was suffering from what would be a constant drain on my creativity and productivity – imposter syndrome. What I didn't then appreciate was *To Be Honest* was my first real step to becoming a novelist. I had done something many writers never achieve – I had finished a first draft. I could, and should, have used that achievement as a way to supercharge my productivity and self-belief. I hadn't yet developed the tools or mindset to do that, but over the years I've formulated an approach to tackle these feelings head on. I now have four steps I try to work through. Give them a try.

**"Writing books is hard.
I think it's important not to get caught
up with the dream of being an author,
and just think, *do you love writing?*
Because ultimately, that's
all you have."**

Charlotte Levin, Episode 197

WRITE HERE, RIGHT NOW

1. **Embrace growth – replace 'I'm not good enough' with 'I'm learning and improving every time I write.'**

2. **Focus on progress, not perfection – replace 'I'll never finish this' with 'Only focus on the next, word, sentence, scene and chapter.'** Every minute you spend adding words to your book, script or story is another step closer to your goals.

3. **Value the process – replace 'This idea is terrible' with 'I'm enjoying myself and everything starts with a messy first draft.'**

4. **Write for yourself – replace 'No one will care about my story' with 'I'm writing for myself first.'** If an audience is there later, great.

3
Writing Sets You Free

Dig your own escape tunnel

> "I became a flight attendant. And I kind of looked at my job and was like, oh, you're going to be a flight attendant for the rest of your life... so I was already getting burnt out by that after a year or two. I was thinking, *I want to pursue the thing that I always said I was going to pursue.*"
>
> Rebecca Thorne, Episode 252

Have you ever felt trapped in a job, career or lifestyle? Do you dream of being able to write full-time, or at least have more time to spend on your creative pursuits? Maybe that's how you feel right now as you read this book. Often, we look at these things as huge, insurmountable obstacles that require a single life-changing decision or event to allow us to break free. But looking at it like that only leads to despair and inertia. We feel hopeless and, as a result, we stop trying. I learned to look at it differently and that's how I eventually turned things around. So can you. Here's how to change your mindset and escape.

A bad sitcom

By now, I was in my mid-twenties and working as a trainee bank manager. It almost sounds like a clichéd set-up for a TV sitcom. I was happy at home, spending time with my wife and baby daughter, but creatively, I was withering on the vine. After a few years at the bank, trying and failing to sell credit cards and loans to people I knew couldn't afford them, the rot set in. I hated my job and longed to do something creative but just couldn't see a way out. I'd talked with my wife about changing careers again, but what was the point? With my experience, lack of formal education and CV, it was only ever likely to be another job in a similar environment, no doubt selling a product or service I didn't believe in. I hadn't written anything for a couple of years but the itch to do something creative and take control of my destiny was building again. I was still writing the occasional song but, like a kettle coming to the boil, the pressure was rising for me to get back to fiction. Aside from the enjoyment, I also instinctively felt writing was my way to discovering what I actually wanted to do with my life, even if I didn't have a clue how that might happen. In the past, this sense of futility prevented me from returning to the blank page, but slowly my mindset was starting to change.

I'm not sure I was even consciously aware of it, until one day, I slipped into one of the offices at work and did something I'd never done before. I locked the door behind me. These offices were in the main banking hall and designed for sales interviews with customers, but when footflow was low, we were expected to make sales calls to try to generate business. There was a small porthole in the door, for staff security (or to check you were actually doing some work). Crucially, the computer screen couldn't be seen by anyone except me. So, I opened up the word processor and began to type. It was a strange, surreal bit of flash fiction about a man who had all the knowledge that has ever existed, trapped inside his head. One day it bursts out as a blinding explosion of light. Looking back, it was clearly a flimsy metaphor for feeling like I had something to say, the need to release some of that creative steam. The whole time I was writing, I was aware I could be interrupted at any moment. Also, unless I wanted to lose my job, I couldn't save the story to the work server. The only way I could preserve what I'd written was to print it as quickly as possible and then delete everything on the screen, which is what I did.

This became my new obsession, stealing small blocks of time to get my writing fix. Soon, after my wife and daughter had gone to sleep, I started to write more short stories at home. It was exhilarating, and even though I still wasn't sure if it was going to lead to anything, it gave me purpose and reminded me of my love for writing. I've learned that to be truly happy I have to be 'making stuff'. Books, songs, films – it always comes back to writing – but that's what keeps me sane and gives me hope.

"The whole point of writing was because you're having the most fun with these worlds and these stories."

Lillian Li, Episode 99

It's the hope that kills you

Hope. They say that's what kills you, but that's bullshit. Hope saves you. At the time, I was scrabbling around for a metaphor that would help me think about my life and future in a different way. How could I escape? That was the question that did it. How *do* you escape? Well, according to every prison break film I'd ever watched, you dig a tunnel. Whether it was the captives in *The Great Escape* or Andy Dufresne in *The Shawshank Redemption*, they slowly and patiently scraped away at the earth, built a tunnel and got the hell out of there. I mean, admittedly, many of the real-life escapees from The Great Escape were captured or killed, but why even mention that? Let's keep things light and positive. Did I know what was on the other side of the wall or exactly how I would get there? No. But if I didn't at least start digging, I was never going to leave my cell. I knew that if writing really was my trusty shovel, I needed to start putting my back into the work again.

"The difference between those who make it and those who don't, is if you are prepared to do the work. That's what it takes."

Tove Alsterdal, Episode 211

The habit was awakened. I wrote every day. Even if I only managed to cram in fifteen minutes, it made me feel better and I could sense my skills sharpening up. I started buying a writing magazine every month and taking out as many books on the subject from the library as I could. Did that nagging voice in the back of my head go completely silent? No. But every time it began to whisper its negativity, I would quieten it with some time at the page. At this point I was writing short stories, sharing them with my friends and family and occasionally entering some of them into competitions. I wasn't finding any success, but it didn't matter. In reality, I wasn't writing for anyone but myself – something I've learned is an essential part of any successful writing journey. I picked up tips and inspiration from books, but I was learning from *doing*. The most effective way to develop your craft is to put in the hours.

I still didn't yet know how I would change my life, but I'd started digging the tunnel that would eventually lead me to the light and the fresh air on the other side of those walls. This single change of mindset was my first real positive step towards a full-time creative career. It would still take many years to dig my way out, but if I hadn't started chipping away at the hard ground, I might still be there now. Who knows how long *your* tunnel might be? So pick up that shovel and dig, dig, dig.

"Well, I'd say you're never too old. I mean, if you think about it, when you're in your 20s, you don't know how long you've got left, do you? Your life could be taken at any time.

There is no guarantee of longevity for anybody. So just because you're 50, 60, 70 or 80, you don't know how long you've got. And therefore, the only time you have is right now.

And if you want to write, then you should write."

Lesley Kara, Episode 255

WRITE HERE, WRITE NOW

1. **Design your own creative escape plan.**
   You don't have to commit to writing every day. Choose something that's achievable and CONSISTENT. Can you set a target of three writing sessions a week? How about a word count target? Yes, real life happens, but sometimes it's too easy to blame external factors on your lack of progress, productivity or motivation. Maybe the escape tunnel metaphor doesn't work for you? No problem. Find an equivalent and tap into something that fires you up, without seeming too daunting.

2. **Go step by step.** Whatever it is, it should help you to break things down into small chunks. Look at what you can do right now, to get you moving in the right direction. You don't need to know the destination, just start the journey. Stop looking for excuses and start writing. Every story starts with a single word. Go write it.

4
Finding Your Process

How do I write?

> "I've got beautiful notepads ready for me to plot. Can't do it. The only way I can do it, is like driving in fog. You know, you start driving and then you clear a little bit, and you keep clearing. I don't know what happens in chapter two until I've written chapter one."
>
> Milly Johnson, Episode 223

Some people say, 'To dissect something is to kill it.' I think this can be true of certain things – comedy, musical inspiration… frogs. But if you're serious about improving your craft, it helps to work out what works and what doesn't. It's like golf. You might miss the ball ten times and then hit a 300-yard drive. If you want to repeat that consistently, it's important to think about (or record) how you did it. Golfers often film their swing and play it back in slow motion, or ask a coach to watch them hit the ball. In this chapter we'll look at how you can find the swing that works for you, so you have more chance of landing on the fairway and getting those words down. I have no idea why I've settled on this golf analogy as I don't even play the game. Let's move on quickly, before anyone notices. Fore!

I need an audience

Now I'd decided on an escape plan, I knew I had to commit

to writing as much as possible. It was sometimes tricky to find the time and the energy, but I squeezed it in wherever I could. At this point I was writing short stories – sometimes getting most of the story down in a single session. I predominantly wrote at night, once my daughter and wife had gone to sleep. This was out of necessity, but I've since discovered I'm most productive in the morning. Back then, I was younger, with more energy, and because I was writing shorter fiction, it was easier to complete ideas quickly and move on to the next thing.

I was enjoying myself, finding my voice and quietly sending some of these stories to close friends and family. It wasn't objective feedback – most of them were too kind to say anything negative – but it did encourage me to keep going. I've always been more productive when I know there's at least one person waiting to read my words. This is one of the many things I've discovered about my process and what motivates me. Now I consciously lean into that.

Bolstered by this feedback and the fact I seemed to have found my motivation again, I decided to try to write another novel. At the time, I was heavily into Douglas Adams. I had always been a fan of *The Hitchhiker's Guide to the Galaxy*, but now I discovered his *Dirk Gently* books, centred around an 'holistic' detective. I loved the humour, atmosphere and originality Adams brought to the long-established detective genre. I began to write a book called *Let Sleeping Gods Lie*. It's about an inept, overweight man who dies and is now stuck in between heaven and hell in a dull administrative office complex called 'Central'. He's a collector of souls, charged with going back to earth to collect recently deceased people and bring them back to Central for processing. Except he's addicted to sausage rolls and is terrible at his job. I think I may have been drawing on my real life again.

I took off at breakneck speed, having no real idea of what would happen. I had a premise, an interesting main character and an itch to write a novel. I would come to learn this approach is called 'flying by the seat of your pants' or 'pantsing', but back then I didn't know there was any other way to do it.

My first beta reader

As I'd discovered I work better when I know someone is actually going to read the book, I was wondering who the lucky person was going to be this time. Many years later, I discovered the term 'beta reader', describing someone willing to read an early draft, or work-in-progress version of your book. Nowadays, there are online groups and other ways to find beta readers, but I found mine in the strangest of places – at work, the job I hated. I was still working at the bank, now in a different, smaller branch, on the outskirts of town. There were only a handful of front office staff, which meant I often got the small staff room upstairs to myself. I started taking my laptop to work and spending my lunch hour happily typing away on my new project. Even on the days when another member of staff appeared, I didn't let it get in the way of my mission.

One day, one of the ladies who worked on the main counter came up for her lunch. Most people weren't really interested in what I was doing. They knew I was one of those 'head-in-the-clouds, artsy-fartsy' types – which was just one of the reasons my sales figures were so bad – so they left me alone. However, Sue, the lady who came up that day, was different. For one thing, unlike many of the other staff, she was a reader. She always had a different novel on the go, often different genres, and was clearly a book worm.

'So, what are you writing?' she asked.

I blinked a couple of times, while I decided whether to be honest with her. It wasn't the first time someone had questioned me, but they were usually bemused I seemed to be doing some kind of 'homework' on my lunch hour. Sue was genuinely interested.

'A novel. I think…' was my tentative answer.

Saying it out loud, it felt strange and embarrassing. I braced myself for either mockery or mild indifference.

'Really?' Sue asked, putting down her own book and showing more interest in me than the entire time I had worked there. 'What's it about?'

She didn't take the piss, roll her eyes or show any signs of cynicism, so I made a snap decision and decided to try to tell her. Bear in mind I hadn't told anyone about the book yet. My wife knew I was writing something, but not what it was. I hadn't even attempted to formulate a pitch for the novel, or really even considered what genre it was. Either way, I was pretty sure it wouldn't be Sue's kind of book. Still, I took a deep breath and gave her a stuttered, mumbling elevator pitch. The elevator must have been in the world's tallest building, because it took me about ten minutes trying to sum it up for her before she finally interrupted me.

'Can I read it?' she asked.

I was stunned. 'What? When I've finished it, you mean?'

'No. Can I read what you've done so far?'

I didn't know how to respond. I know there will be writers reading this screaming at me to say no to this poor, naive woman. What fool would share a first draft, let alone a zero draft, like the one I was writing? I didn't even know how the story was going to end. To be honest, I wasn't that certain of what would happen in the next chapter. I would be mad to let her read it at this stage. It was a non-starter. Only an idiot would cave in.

'Yes. Alright,' I told her.

So, with trepidation, and lots of caveats, I emailed her the first chapter. I told her to be as honest as she wanted and to tell me if it wasn't her bag.

'Read it!' she told me excitedly, the very next day. 'Can I read the next chapter?'

Sue was originally from the North and wasn't given to blowing smoke up people's backsides – giving false compliments, I mean. I knew if she didn't like it, she definitely wouldn't be asking to read more of it. She told me that even though it wasn't the kind of thing she would usually read, she thought it was funny and really wanted to know what happened next. I was stunned and elated. Finally, someone outside of my circle of family and friends was showing an interest in my work. So, for the next few weeks, I sent her a chapter every few days. Eventually, Sue caught up and was having to wait for me to write the next one. This only pushed me to write faster. She asked me questions about the characters, told me her favourite bits and was both enthusiastic and supportive.

The King of writing books

Having Sue hot on my heels was both a blessing and a curse. On the positive side of things, I was writing more than I had for years, and at a rate I hadn't ever reached before. I was fired-up and excited about this new world I was creating and was racing to finish it. But that's where the trouble began. How exactly was I going to end the story?

I was slowing down and the gaps between chapters were starting to get longer and longer. Sue was still asking for more chapters, but I think even she could sense I was losing momentum and she became less insistent, seeing I was becoming uncomfortable. When I was transferred to another branch, and lost my cheerleader, the book ground to a halt and I wasn't sure what to do. I went back to writing short stories and then one day, whilst browsing in a bookshop I stumbled on what would become my favourite book about writing.

> **"I haven't done any writing courses, or read many 'how to write a novel' books, but I did read *On Writing* by Stephen King over and over again. I love that book so much. I really recommend it."**
>
> Will Dean, Episode 109

Stephen King's part-memoir, part-inspirational instruction manual has been mentioned more times on the podcast than any other book – and with good reason. I devoured it and, finally, I began to understand what it really meant to be a writer. This was where I truly learned about editing and revision. The idea of writing the first draft with the door closed and the second draft with the door open. The first version of the book is allowed to be terrible. It's your way of getting the story out and discovering what it is you're really writing about. King is very much in the 'pantser' (writing by the seat of his pants) camp and loves the fact he has no idea what's going to happen. His rationale is how can the reader guess where the story is headed, if he has no idea when he's writing it? This was when I started to seriously think about my process.

"I think if you can get to the end of a first
draft, that's a massive, massive achievement…
I think that's the hardest thing."

CJ Tudor, Episode 77

"What doesn't work for me is just starting to
write… without knowing where I'm going…
that is very, very bad advice for me."

Merle Nyegate, Episode 97

As impressed and influenced as I was by *On Writing*, I immediately understood that just because that's the way Stephen King did it, it might not be the right way for me. This instinct has been proven correct over a decade of speaking to other writers. Each author I've interviewed has their own unique method and what I've come to realise is that there is no one right way to write a novel – only the right way for *you* to write *your* novel.

I knew if I wanted to improve, I needed to consciously think about my process. I began to keep a writing journal. It wasn't in-depth or pages long, just a few lines after each writing session to say how it went. I recorded the number of words I'd written, but also how I felt. Did the words come easy? Were they forced? How long did it take to reach that amount of words? Was I distracted? I also made a note of what time of day I was doing the work. I soon realised that, for me, my most productive time was the morning. Whilst I knew I wouldn't always be able to get the words down in the morning, because of work and having a young daughter, I made it a priority to try to make it happen. That often meant getting up an hour earlier than everyone else and doing the writing before I went to work. This is something that's remained with me now, years later, and I aim to get to my laptop as early as possible. For you, it might be late at night, when everyone has gone to bed, or stealing some time on your lunch hour. It doesn't matter. Find what works for you. That begins with noticing the way you do it now and formalising it as much as you can.

Keeping a writing journal was a game changer for me. By consciously looking at how I wrote, and what worked best, I was able to attain something that had so far eluded me: CONSISTENCY. I was developing muscle memory, a routine, until it became second nature to sit at my laptop and get the words down.

As for *Let Sleeping Gods Lie*, that first half-finished version of the book is lost to the mists of time, but I loved the premise and knew I had to find a way to write it. I would eventually find my way back to it – and this time get to the end. More on that later.

WRITE HERE, WRITE NOW

1. **Start a writing journal.** Work out how you write. What's your process? When do you do it? How do you do it? What works best? Maybe you like to write your first draft by hand and then type it up? Have you got a particular place you like to go? What tends to distract you or make it hard to get the words down? Does it help or hinder you to have a word target, for example? Are short bursts, or big chunks of time more effective?

2. **Mix it up.** Use the journal to try different approaches. It's not something you need to do forever, but whether you're a relatively new writer or someone with years of experience behind you, we all get stuck in a rut from time to time. This is a simple way to take stock, find new ways of working and a process that works for you.

5
Side Quests

Let life lead you somewhere new

> "Make sure you've got stuff to write about. Don't just write books that are like books you've read. Make sure you do some living first."
>
> John Lincoln, Episode 100

This chapter, true to its name and subject, will feel like a side quest, as we step away from the strictly chronological structure to talk about my foray into filmmaking and its impact on my creative life. You may feel you're currently on your own side quest, toiling away in a career you hate, or perhaps thinking your other non-writing activities aren't helping you to progress with your books and stories. By the end of the chapter, you'll understand how bringing other forms of creativity – or even different skills from your day job – can supercharge your writing and add more depth to your work.

"I've spent quite a substantial amount of my adult life working abroad and observing people. Maybe that comes through in the narrator as well."

Rosanna Amaka, Episode 119

Silver screen dreams

You could argue I've had many side quests in my life but the one that's had the most impact on my self-confidence and, eventually my journey to publication, has been filmmaking. Back in my late twenties, aside from chipping away at my writing, and noodling away writing songs, I started to explore another passion I've had since I was a kid: film.

My love of fiction came from my mum, but my interest in films and TV was inspired by my dad. I saw my first film at the cinema when I was three years old. I remember sitting spellbound, watching the 'the big telly', as my dad had described it beforehand. The film was *Flash Gordon* – hardly a classic – but I was immediately hooked. From an early age, Dad gave me an education, as I sat beside him watching everything from Ealing comedies to classic westerns and influential crime films like *Angels with Dirty Faces*. The latter blew me away with its powerful and ambiguous ending. No spoilers – although it was made in 1938! – but if you haven't seen it, try to get a copy, because it's great storytelling.

In exactly the same way I'd read books beyond my age, it wasn't long before I was watching films I probably shouldn't have gone near until I was well into my teens. Films like *The Terminator, The Killing Fields* and what is still my favourite film to this day: *The Godfather*. I was blown away by the sheer scope of the story, its nuanced characters. There was no black and white – only shades of grey. Even now, this idea heavily influences my writing. Whiter-than-white protagonists bore me.

Unlike my dad, I became obsessed with reading the

credits after the film ended. Remember, this was a time long before the internet and Wikipedia. I was always fascinated to discover who had written and directed the film. It became a way for me to seek out other films by the same creatives and fuelled a desire to learn about how films were put together. I found books in the library and hoovered up everything I could find on the subject. It was an obsession, but at that point I hadn't even considered the idea of writing scripts or becoming a director.

That all changed when I was sixteen and Quentin Tarantino released *Reservoir Dogs* and inspired a bunch of other films with fast-paced, hip dialogue and his distinctive shooting style. When he followed it up with *Pulp Fiction*, a friend and I became convinced we could and should write a script. We bought a couple of published screenplays so we could learn the format and then got to work writing a short film. It felt good to learn a new skill and have fun bouncing around ideas. That was my first taste of writing dialogue and, although I didn't realise it at the time, my introduction to the concept of 'show, don't tell'. But without an obvious way to turn our script into a film, the idea eventually fizzled out, and we began to think more generally about writing sketches that could be performed on stage. Which is how I ended up writing the sketches for the show I put on in the sixth form.

"I worked for the BBC for five years, commissioning comedy, which was a fantastic job because it meant I had to read a lot of scripts and say why they're working or not working."

Merle Nyegate, Episode 97

Action!

Years later, on the back of my new 'escape tunnel' momentum, I circled back to my filmmaking aspirations. I bought a cheap camcorder, a rickety tripod and some basic editing software for my computer. I started off filming and editing simple family videos, adding music and text and entertaining my loved ones with these fun short films. As I got more ambitious, I decided to try my hand at making music videos for other bands. I'd seen how it was done when my friend Rich – who was also my original scriptwriting buddy – made a video for my band. He brought along Matt, a colleague from his job at a local video production company.

Although I had no formal qualifications or experience, Matt must have recognised my ambition and willingness to learn because, a few years later when he decided to start his own production company, he would eventually offer me a job. I had the opportunity to edit lots of short 'talking heads' videos, taking a bunch of footage from one or more interviews and cutting them down to punchy two-minute videos. This was a great way to learn the basics of video editing, but has also helped me massively with my writing. Knowing how to get to the crux of a scene as efficiently as possible is a big advantage, and one of the reasons I now enjoy editing a book as much as writing it.

Despite starting out in corporate video production, Matt and I eventually moved on to making more artistically rewarding films. We've made films about writers, artists, instrument makers and all kinds of other creatives. We went on to produce an award-winning feature-length documentary called *No Fare: The Sian Green Story*, which again helped me to craft an over-arching narrative. I learned about the three-act structure and eventually returned to my aspiration to write screenplays. I've now written and directed several short films, including *INKLING*, a film that started out as a short story and went on to be an official selection at the HorrorHound Film Festival in Ohio.

All of this helped me in practical ways I could apply to my novel writing. For example, the concept of 'come in late, get out early' – starting a scene at the last possible moment, when it's relevant to your reader or audience – and ending it, or 'getting out', as soon as you've hit the story beat you're aiming for. You can also apply it to the wider narrative. How many of us find we've started our books a few chapters too early, while we cover lots of back-story? I know I have. Bring us straight into the middle of the action and the audience will find their feet as they go. There are loads of other techniques I've transferred over to my prose writing, including scene structure and character development. I've also taken the advice from well-known screenwriting books, like Blake Snyder's *Save The Cat* and incorporated it into my book-writing process. I went on to create a workshop to help other novelists apply the same techniques.

The bigger picture – pun intended – was that this side quest didn't only increase the size of my writing toolbox. Eventually I was lucky I was able to turn one of my creative passions into a career, but even if filmmaking hadn't become my job, I firmly believe we need to nurture other artistic pursuits and interests. Julia Cameron and others have described it as "filling our creative well". She talks of taking yourself on an artist's date, very specifically arranging a solo outing or time to nurture your artistic side. I love that idea, but think you should also apply it more generally to your life and writing and to think more laterally. The artistic side of things is important, but even without these side quests, I believe you can – and should – be looking for skills and qualities you can transfer to your writing. Even if you think your day job is dry and boring, there will be aspects of your experiences and training that will help you become a better, more productive writer.

"Well, the number one thing is just a real natural curiosity to understand and learn as much as possible. I knew how to research something. I was fearless about calling people up and asking for information."

Mark Stevens, Episode 208

WRITE HERE, WRITE NOW

1. **Think about your own side quests.** Everyone has detours in their lives. Some creative, some not. Think about how you might be able to take the skills you learned there and bring them to your writing journey.

2. **Look beyond writing.** It might be the patience you've gained from learning an intricate skill. Were you a project manager? Do you work in a fast-paced business environment? Bring those organisational strengths to how you write – schedule in your writing sessions or introduce more planning to your work. Have you worked in a customer-facing job? Think about all the characters you met along the way and the stories you can steal.

3. **Embrace a new side quest – it's never too late.** If you don't think any of those are relevant, why not try a new side quest? Find a different creative avenue to explore or try writing in a different medium, like screenwriting or a radio play.

6
Get Going and Don't Stop

Momentum and focus

> "I'm a firm believer that momentum helps when you're writing. You know, if you're writing in fits and starts, doing 1,000 words one week and leaving it three, four weeks and then coming back to it, it's harder."
>
> Dan Howarth, Episode 155

Starting a book or story is easy. You're filled with the energy, excitement and inspiration that comes with a new idea. Sometimes this feeling lasts months, sometimes it lasts hours, but it can be hard to maintain when the project is vague or open-ended. If you're ever going to actually finish that first draft, you have to see it through to completion and the key to that is often momentum. Stopping for any length of time leaves a gap for insecurity to sneak in again and before you know it, the idea of trying to pick up where you left off can seem too daunting. This chapter will give you tips to get going and keep going, until that first draft is finished.

"Normally I write probably 2,000 words each day, but when it gets close to deadline I'm on more like 5,000 or 6,000 words a day and it's absolutely intense."

Helen Cooper, Episode 220

If at first you don't succeed

Remember that novel, *Let Sleeping Gods Lie,* I told you about? The one I lost faith in? I loved the premise of the book and couldn't shake off my main character, Eddie Vaulter. Months after I'd stopped writing the book, Eddie and the story would taunt me, leaving me unable to get away from the feeling of failure and regret. I just couldn't face going back to that abandoned draft after such a long time. Does any of this sound familiar? Have you struggled to find your way back into a project?

As I pondered a solution, I discovered NaNoWriMo, or National Novel Writing Month. For those unfamiliar with 'NaNo', as it was always affectionately known, it was an annual writing challenge to write at least 50,000 words of a novel during the month of November. There was a great online community you could join and, if you wanted some in-person encouragement, even local 'chapters' or groups that met at cafes in your town.

I wasn't going to 'cheat' and go back to my original draft of the book. For one thing, the whole point was to start fresh and get a new perspective, but I also wanted to see if I could start from scratch again and prove myself. I didn't even re-read the old version. I opened a new Word document, cracked my knuckles – in the way they do at the start of every clichéd writing or fighting montage you've ever seen – and prepared to begin a brand-new draft.

50,000 words in a month sounds crazy – and in many ways it is! – but like anything, the key is to break it down into manageable chunks. The reality means having to write around 1,600 words every day for the entire month. Each day I had to input my word total online and watch as I inched towards my target. Some days it was a struggle, having to write late into the night, just to drag myself over the line for that day. At other times, the words came easily and I wrote many more than the 1,666 words required.

I had only decided to take on the challenge a few days before the start of November, but knew that if I wanted to be able to write at such speed, I would need at least the hint of a plan. I didn't have the time – or the will – to plan the whole thing, but I wrote a couple of sentences to describe each upcoming chapter and made sure I could always see at least three chapters in front of me. That way I didn't need to stop writing to think. It was also where I learned the value of an old piece of writing advice, paraphrased perfectly by guest, Angela Ackerman.

"One technique that I'll use to stay in the writing flow, is I'll stop halfway through a scene or knowing exactly where things are going to go next, so that when I return to writing, I don't need to look back."

Angela Ackerman, Episode 58

Whirlwind romance

One of the many benefits of attempting this type of challenge was that I didn't have time to question anything I was writing. No more editing the last paragraph or agonising over a particular sentence or idea. I wrote with joy and abandon, seeing a first draft appear before my eyes at a speed I'd never experienced. Returning to the book day after day also meant I was immersed in the story and characters. I didn't need to over-analyse what they might say or do in any given situation, because I was getting intimately acquainted with them over a short space of time. It was like me and the book were the two leads in a rom-com, thrown together and falling in love in a matter of days.

Even though NaNoWriMo was free to enter, with no other 'prize' except a discount to buy the Scrivener writing software (the tool I'm now using to write this book), it gave me a hard deadline. It also helped that I was running this race with thousands of other writers around the world, all of us with the same goal. To be honest, when I decided to take on the challenge, I'm not sure I really believed I could achieve it, but my attitude was that even if I didn't get to 50,000 words, I would still have written more than I had in a very long time.

It also broke my debilitating habit of editing a book as I went along. Whilst this can work for some writers, in my experience it can make us over-think and kill momentum.

**"I don't have word targets but I use *Scrivener*
and I've got a word count, so I know how much
I have to hit by the end of it. If it's looking
bad towards the end, I've got to speed up."**

William Shaw, Episode 63

It was pedal-to-the-metal writing that kept me at least one step ahead of the malaise that can creep in when we take a more leisurely approach to that first draft. I found other new techniques that I still use when writing my first drafts, like skipping over anything that requires deep thought or research. I simply use square brackets as placeholders. For example, even now, my first drafts contain things like [LOOK UP NAME OF FLOWER] or [FUNNY META-PHOR HERE]. If I can't come up with something within a minute or two, I use a placeholder and move on. Research, in particular, can be a massive time-sap and, even worse, often leads to spending hours down weird and wonderful internet rabbit holes. One minute you're looking up the name of a fancy cheese and the next you're watching a chef giving you three new ways to use Gruyere. Like sharks, we have to keep moving or we die [CHECK SHARK FACT IN NEXT DRAFT]. I use square brackets, but feel free to come up with a system that works for you. Tony Schum-acher had his own unique way of leaving himself remind-ers.

> **"If I get to a part of something where I can't remember a character's name or what car they were driving, I just type 'Oozalum', the name of the bird they hunt in the film, *Carry On Up the Jungle*! It's easy to search for in the edit."**

Tony Schumacher, Episode 69

Write, sleep, repeat

One study showed that, to create a habit, you need to do it at least twenty-one times. With NaNo, I got thirty chances to make writing a daily exercise. It worked and, even now, it feels strange if I go more than a day or two without writing something. When I began the NaNoWriMo challenge, I'm not entirely sure I believed I could hit the 50,000 word target, but it was exhilarating to give it a try. I assumed that as the deadline loomed, I would have to force myself to write for longer periods of time just so I could squeak past the target with 50,001 words at 11.55 p.m. on November 30th. The reality was I sailed past that and as the calendar ticked over to December, I had written more than 60,000 words. I was shocked and elated. I knew writing that amount of words every day for several months in a row wasn't going to be sustainable, but it showed me what I was capable of. And a couple of months later, I completed the entire 90,000-word first draft. It proved I could actually finish the first draft of a full-length book, not just a novella. Until that moment, I realised, I hadn't thought I would ever get to the end of a story that length and write those two glorious words: THE END.

> **"I think no writing is wasted, even if you have ten books that don't get published. The eleventh book that does get published wouldn't have been written if you hadn't written those ten."**

> Laura Pearson, Episode 212

Let Sleeping Gods Lie is still yet to make its way into the world, because it isn't good enough in its current form, but it was another practice book. It was how I learned what I was capable of. It taught me more about crafting a full story arc and how to develop my characters. It gave me the confidence to try again. Through countless podcast interviews, I came to learn this is common for most writers. Even household names with many published books behind them, have usually written several books before they write 'the one' that eventually finds its way into the world. Like any craft, the best way to get better at it, is to do it and see it through to completion.

WRITE HERE, WRITE NOW

1. **Create some momentum.** NaNoWriMo helped me find my writing mojo and create a life-long habit. The official version of NaNo is now defunct, but that doesn't mean you can't set yourself your own version of the challenge or find other ways to kickstart your momentum. Come up with a crazy writing goal and allow yourself to write with total abandon. If you don't want to commit to a big word target, try aiming for a 'writing streak'. How many days in a row can you get to the page and put down some words?

2. **Write now, edit later.** Every time you try to write a book, you learn something about yourself and the craft, so don't spend too long agonising over every word. The goal is to get the full story onto paper. Nothing else matters. It doesn't matter how ugly it is, pull it out into the world and give your novel life. Remember, when it comes to that first draft, to stand still is to die. That means no research tangents or hours spent shaping the perfect sentence. Momentum is your secret weapon, so JUST KEEP MOVING.

7
Build It and They Will Come

Community and accountability

> "If you're a writer, you've got to be in the writing community and writing circles, because other writers are the best people and so supportive and so lovely."
>
> Zoe Lea, Episode 235

There's no getting around it: writing is a solitary pursuit. We sit alone for hours, days, weeks, months and sometimes even years, faces lit by the sickly glow of our laptops as we disappear into our own heads. It's easy to become isolated. When there's no one else around to support you, motivation can crumble. Fortunately, it doesn't have to be that way. This chapter is all about community and how it's not only good for your mental health, but can level-up your skills too.

Finding the tribe

Discovering NaNoWriMo (National Novel Writing Month) had been a slice of luck, but with hindsight it was also because I'd started to tentatively reach out into the world to try to find other writers and creatives. Back then, before a certain tech billionaire took the reins, Twitter was a great place to find like-minded people. You could search the feeds for specific hashtags and topics, and that's how I would eventually find many of the early guests for *The Write Place* podcast. But back then, I was just scrabbling around, looking for bits of writing advice. That's how I'd found NaNo.

But before that, I had no idea how I might find other writers locally. Which, now I come to think about it, makes me look pretty stupid. After all, the internet existed by then. It seems obvious I could have just Googled 'writers in Leicester' or something, but I honestly hadn't considered the idea that groups of writers would exist. I mean, why would they? Writing is something you have to do alone, right? Why would writers be congregating in groups?

"I always describe it as finding a tribe. It's finding the right people, or person, to work with."

Nikki Moore, Episode 232

A few months after NaNoWriMo, I was scrolling through Twitter, looking for tasty writing morsels, when I came across a tweet from a local writer, Maria Smith. I can't remember exactly what the tweet said but it had a link to a blog post she'd written. I clicked through to her post, which was an update of what she had been working on recently and how things were going. It was honest and made all the more interesting because I discovered Maria, like me, was based in Leicestershire. In that post she mentioned a group she belonged to. It was a critique group called Phoenix Writers. My pulse quickened. Critique? Feedback from other people who actually wrote and knew what they were talking about? How did I not know this was a thing? How would it even work? Did they meet in person? When? Where? I had to find out more.

They met on Saturdays, so there wouldn't be any clashes with my day job, and the venue was close and easy to get to. I reached out to Maria and asked how someone would go about joining the group. Maria said I could come along and try out for the group. Try out? So I had to pass some kind of test? Gulp. As it turned out, this wasn't a case of Phoenix Writers being some elitist group trying to keep out the riff-raff. It was really to see if my level of writing was sufficient to get benefit from their critique and also for me to see if the group was a good fit.

The day came and I had to take 1,000 words of my work to read out to the group. Yes – *read out*. I'm used to performing, so it wasn't the thought of standing up in front of a room of strangers which bothered me. It was the idea of reading something I'd written to a bunch of people who might actually know what they were talking about. Still, I was desperate for constructive feedback and knew it was the only way I was going to develop as a writer, so I took the opening chunk of a short story I'd been writing and headed into town.

I've since learned the way Phoenix Writers does it isn't necessarily typical of how other critique groups work. Many groups distribute the words to the group a week or so before the next session so that everyone can make notes and get their thoughts in order. Phoenix didn't send out the work ahead of time, so it was fresh to the ears of the group. This has pros and cons. I've since been in groups that use the other method and, whilst the feedback can sometimes be more in-depth on a line-by-line basis, it often misses a key consideration: how the work lands in the room. When you're reading aloud to an audience, you can sense when something is working, if it falls flat or there's an element of confusion. I regularly read my work out loud when I'm editing – it's a great way to hear clumsy phrasing and spot mistakes. But doing that in front of a room of writers? That takes it to a whole new level. You suddenly become aware of every misplaced word, repetition and anything that screams 'bad writing'. Another pro of the Phoenix method is that, as a listener, you have to really focus on the work of others and practise critical thinking.

"If you go to writing groups, you've got to be able to take some constructive criticism… if you're getting lots of rejections and no one else has read what you've written, then maybe you should be thinking about getting someone else to read it and be able to take on board what you're doing wrong."

Nathan O'Hagan, Episode 50

Everyone's a critic

Before it was my turn to read, there were two or three other readers. We were expected to listen and give feedback. Give feedback?! I hadn't even read out my work yet. At first, I struggled to concentrate, or to even know what to say. So I listened to what the other writers picked out and soon began to get a sense of the things I should be looking for. I had only been there for half an hour and I could already feel my writing world beginning to expand. But now it was finally my turn to read and to take my first dose of critique medicine. I knew from years of performing experience that a side effect of nervous energy is to speak too fast and garble your words, so I took a deep breath and made an effort to read slowly and clearly. I think I managed that side of things, but as I stood there reading my story, my mind was going at a hundred miles an hour. What are they thinking? What if they hate it? What if they hate *me*? Despite this, I held it together, finished reading my allotted 1,000 words and sat down. I opened my notebook and prepared for the worst.

Now, if this was a film, after the set-up I've just given you, the feedback would have been incredibly positive. Writers would be blowing their nose and wiping away their tears as they tried to come to terms with the literary phenomenon that had suddenly entered their midst. Hasty plans would be drawn up to enter me for the Booker Prize and the other writers would be muttering phrases like "he's the new Ian McEwan".

If only.

"There was a lot of over-writing."

"The set-up was OK, but it was too convoluted."

"Some of it was quite good, but I didn't understand the bit where…"

"You switched point of view on the line where you said…"

And on and on it went. There was some positive encouragement, but it was predominantly constructive feedback, as it should be. I've since spoken to other writers about the first time they received real feedback, and they described it as 'crushing' or a 'knock to their confidence' but for me, it was a revelation. It's no exaggeration to say I learned more about writing in those ten minutes of feedback than I had learned in the previous ten years of writing in isolation. I still think of that day as the single biggest leap forward in my skills as a writer. And I soon discovered it wasn't just receiving critique on my own work that helped me grow, but listening to the work of others and being able to think critically about any piece of writing, regardless of genre, style or the level they were at. I learned just as much from novice writers as I did from more seasoned members. It taught me how to give and receive feedback. Here's what I learned.

When giving feedback, remember:

- **Be polite and respectful at all times.**

- **Don't get personal.**

- **Give specific examples.**

- **Don't make plot suggestions unless asked.**

- **Find something positive to include.**

- **Ask questions if needed.**

When receiving feedback:

- **Listen to, and write down, every point or suggestion during an in-person critique session, even if you instinctively disagree with it or have reservations about the person delivering** it.

- **Be professional and let go of any baggage you may have about the critic's experience, knowledge or motives.**

- **Take time to process the feedback and look for consensus among multiple critics.**

- **Don't get defensive or argue.** If the critic asks for an explanation, calmly make your argument.

- **If it's written critique, resist the temptation to fire off an angry email reply.**

- **Consider all the critique, but don't act on every suggestion or comment.**

- **If more than one person makes different comments about the same passage or sentence, it usually means there's *something* wrong with it.** It's up to you to take a closer look and work out exactly what that might be.

"It's much easier to see weaknesses in other people's novels than your own. It is an independent task to write a novel, but you do rely on other people as well. So there's collaboration that goes on, which is so valuable."

Gail Aldwin, Episode 143

Whether giving or receiving feedback, remember the main purpose of a good critique group is to create a safe space, a supportive environment in which all members can develop and flourish. You're in this together. The more each of you develops their craft, the stronger the group becomes and the greater the benefits for all.

I appreciate it may not be practical, or even desirable for some of us introverts to find a group to join. If that's the case, at least try to find one other writer you can share your work with. In return, read and critique their stuff. You can still learn from each other and gain knowledge and confidence.

Treat feedback as a gift. Like any gift, it's rude to throw it back in the face of the person who gave it to you, but that doesn't mean you have to keep it. It's your work and you have to decide which bits of critique you take on board. In my experience, the more open-minded you are, the more you can improve your work. Accept it with gratitude and humility and before you dismiss it out of hand, give yourself time to consider it. It takes a while to realise whose opinion you trust, but whoever you listen to, don't lose sight of your original voice and vision.

"You know, I've been in the same writing group for the last twelve years and I would not be published without them."

Scott Reintgen, Episode 157

WRITE HERE, WRITE NOW

1. **Find one writing ally or group.**

2. **Don't forget, it's a two-way street.**
   Make sure you reciprocate – read and give feedback on the work of others too. Be brave, share your work and learn to deal with feedback.

3. **Remember, it's not personal.**
   Whether traditionally published or not, you will need to get used to feedback and re-writing. Which leads us nicely on to our next topic, ~~revision~~ re-writing.

8
The Long Game

Writing is re-writing and
getting unstuck

> "You're going to be re-writing this later anyway. Just stop being precious and stop trying to write the perfect first draft, you fool!"
>
> D.V. Bishop, Episode 237

Even if you're just starting out, there's a good chance you've heard the maxim 'writing is re-writing'. When I first stumbled across this piece of wisdom – possibly in *On Writing*, again – I thought, sure, of course I'll have to re-write the odd sentence here and there. Maybe even change some paragraphs. But the possibility of re-writing an entire story or novel? Come now. Surely not? But the fact is, if you're serious about finding and keeping an audience for your work, you have to come to terms with the notion that, sometimes, you really do have to rip it up and start again. It certainly took me a while to get my head around it, so let's look at how you can change your mindset too.

The long and winding road

I began writing the book that would eventually become my debut novel, *Safe Hands*, in October of 2015. It would take at least another six years until I had a publishable version and eight years in total, until it was finally in print. Would I have started it if I'd known how long the path to publication would be? Best not to think about that right now.

Safe Hands began as a short story, with a working title

of 'Cops and Robbers'. My general idea was to write a totally unapologetic, flint-hard protagonist, seemingly without any real redeeming features, other than he was very, very good at his job. He was Mickey Blake, an expert safecracker with a heightened sense of touch and a gift for sarcasm. My inspiration was Richard Stark's Parker character – a ruthless criminal, with no apparent backstory or emotional depth and yet compelling enough to spawn a long series of books and several films. Parker has an uncompromising professional code, a sharp wit and is the best at what he does. I've always been influenced by American crime writers like George Pelicanos, Dennis Lehane and Elmore Leonard, but I wanted to put a more grounded, British spin on the genre.

As the original plan was to write a short story, I went out of my way to make Mickey as uncompromising, irreverent and funny as I could. The early pages I took to Phoenix Writers were well received and got lots of laughs, which perhaps spurred me on. But the real fuel for my productivity was the fact I was falling in love with writing the character of Mickey Blake. Before *Safe Hands*, I rarely wrote from a first-person perspective ('I did this, I saw that', etc.), but once I had Mickey's voice in my head, I couldn't see any other way to do it. He spoke to me and I wrote it down, warts and all. It was liberating. That original version of Mickey was about as far away from the real me as it was possible to be. Maybe that's why I was finding it such fun. After a few thousand words, I knew Mickey needed his own book. To paraphrase the film *Withnail and I* – I seemed to have started a novel by mistake.

"It is the essence of good writing that you care about the character. There are ways to make the reader care and otherwise, in a novel, you just won't turn the page."

Bonnie MacBird, Episode 68

Whilst the snippets I was reading in my critique group were landing well and my scenes were entertaining, I wasn't paying enough attention to character development. Using Parker as an inspiration for Mickey was fine, but I had to accept that Stark's character was created in the 1960s, when attitudes to women were perhaps not as progressive as they are now. Actually, that's an understatement. This was the era of Connery's Bond, where it was seen as being perfectly natural to slap a woman when she was being 'hysterical'. Sex could be demanded and members of the opposite sex were seen as disposable trophies on the way to the hero's eventual triumph. These films and characters were very much of their time, although attitudes didn't really start to change until relatively recently. Aside from the sexism, many of those characters were one dimensional, lacking any emotional depth or complexity. Don't get me wrong, those characters still exist in films, TV and books today, but that wasn't the kind of book I wanted to write. My aim was always to have Mickey follow an arc and to change over the course of the novel. However, it soon became clear that the way Mickey came across in the opening chapters of my first draft was actively discouraging female readers, in particular, from reading the rest of the book. This is why re-writing and listening to critique is so important.

> **"A question that comes up often – is a scene or chapter moving the central plot forward? There can be passages or chapters where they're beautifully done, but are they contributing to the thrust of the novel?"**

Clio Cornish, Editor, Episode 89

Where am I going?

There were a number of factors that helped me to better shape both the novel and Mickey's character. The first was actually deciding how the book was to end. As a pantser at the time, this seemed impossible to me, without writing the whole thing. However, now it's something I would advise everyone to try to do. Perhaps you don't need to know when you begin the novel, but by the time you hit your midpoint, you really do need to know what the end game is – even if you're not quite sure how to get there. I won't give you any spoilers, but the climax of *Safe Hands* involves breaking into a vault. For me, the key (pun intended) was to know what would be inside, when and if it was opened. Once I decided that, everything slotted into place and it also helped me add more emotional depth to Mickey.

The next piece of the puzzle came when I joined a new critique group. This one was formed by Ericka Waller. It was online and was aimed more at novelists who could share longer sections of their work with a small group of writers, over several weeks and months. It meant they got a sense of the entire book and character arcs, rather than focusing on single scenes or chapters. It was a group full of talented authors, including Ericka, S.J. Watson and Sarah Bonner.

Ericka made two suggestions which would finally unlock my quandary and vastly improve the novel. The first was to focus on Mickey's real unique gift – his hands. If he could feel every nuance within a huge vault door, why wasn't his experience of the world in general coloured by this heightened perception? It was a game-changer. It allowed me to get into Mickey's head in a way that I hadn't previously been able to do. It stripped away an outer layer of his character to let the reader see just how sensitive Mickey actually was.

Her second suggestion was to see if I could try writing from the perspective of my main female character. In the original version, Mickey was the only point of view (POV) character in the book. I was initially sceptical but, now embracing my 'writing is re-writing' mantra, I gave it a try and was shocked to discover not only did I really enjoy writing Hazel as a POV character, but it radically changed the story for the better. Now I had a convincing subplot that added real depth and made the book more accessible to a female audience. If someone had suggested such huge changes to me even a few months earlier, I'm not sure I would have found the strength to essentially 'break' the novel I had written. Even when I began to make the changes Ericka and the group had suggested, I was still reticent to start from scratch. I tried to edit and amend existing chapters to slot in some of the 'hands' stuff. I tweaked other scenes to try to shoehorn them into being from Hazel's perspective.

Ericka and the group spotted this a mile away. They said the difference between an existing chapter and a new scene written with their changes in mind was night and day. But how could I throw away almost an entire novel to basically start again? I wrestled with it for another few weeks before I was finally ready to face the truth: I was going to have to re-write the whole bloody thing. Ugh. So that's what I did. I dragged almost all of the chapters into a folder I created called 'Offcuts and Maybes' (a way of giving myself the delusion that I might be able to keep some stuff) and began the re-write in earnest.

The strange thing was I wrote that draft in a matter of a few months, because now I knew my characters inside out. I had a new angle for Mickey and a brand-new perspective for Hazel. Of course, that draft wasn't my final version either, but it was much closer. I was approaching the end of my marathon… or so I thought.

"The main thing is people don't do it enough times. They write that first draft and then they'll go through it once. They'll re-read it and aimlessly re-write sentences and that's not a good strategy. So I tend to say before you even consider submission, go through it three times, with purpose."

Liam J. Cross, Editor, Episode 93

"I just move these chess pieces around. If I'm stuck on something in the plot there's nothing like imagining what it would be like as a TV show or a film, because it really cuts to the chase of what you should get to quickly, rather than all the redundant material that's slowing you down."

Ruth Kelly, Episode 205

WRITE HERE, WRITE NOW

1. **Embrace the re-write.** If you're stuck or crawling along in the dark, try turning your novel on its head.

2. **Ask yourself, 'Am I writing in the best POV for my character or book?'** Is it third-person — he, she, they, for example? If so, try on first-person for size. Does it change how your character behaves, or how you feel about them?

3. **Dig deeper into your character.** What makes them tick? Does it add depth to your story or suggest new plot threads?

4. **Try adding a new POV character, like I did.**

5. **Blow it up.** When Stephen King got stuck in the middle of *The Stand*, he killed half the characters! Can you do something as drastic to shake things up?

6. **Don't abandon the book.** Change things up and remember that the best version of your book is buried in the re-write.

9
Dealing with Rejection

It ain't over 'til it's over

> "If you want to do this, particularly if you want to do it for a living, you have to be very tenacious and you have to have a philosophy about rejection."
>
> Tosca Lee, Episode 84

No.

One word you must get used to hearing. Again and again and again. Imagine 'no' to be your least favourite food. Maybe it's Brussell sprouts or Marmite on toast, liver and onions or porridge made with water (shudders). For me it would be tripe. For the uninitiated, tripe is the lining of a cow's stomach. It's like trying to eat a bicycle inner tube and probably tastes worse. My grandma regularly tried to make me eat it as a child. The point is, whatever your version of tripe is… get ready to eat plates and plates of the stuff before you even get a sniff of dessert. This is the life of a writer, or any artist, trying to get past gatekeepers to find an audience for their work. Like anything, if you eat enough, you will grow to tolerate it – maybe even enjoy it? Well, let's not go that far, but you will at least be able to digest it and with each forkful, you'll be that much closer to that delicious sticky toffee pudding called 'success'.

And with yet another tortuous metaphor, we find ourselves talking about rejection. If you are to get your words out into the world, it's something you'll have to endure. Too many writers fall by the wayside, even when success might be just around the corner. In this chapter, I'll talk you through the nuts and bolts of the submissions process and you'll see perseverance is the key, even when it seems all hope is lost.

The dreaded submission

**"It really is quite simple...
It's something I cannot stop reading.
I want a reason to read on."**

Madeleine Milburn, Literary Agent, Episode 38

Armed with the shiny new version of my book and more optimism than a Labrador puppy with a new toy, I began to prepare my submissions package for *Safe Hands*. This varies depending on the guidelines of each agent or publisher but as a general rule, here's what we have to put together:

- **A covering letter.**
  For probably twenty years now, this has been a 'covering email' but for some reason no one calls it that. It's a short, well-written email that gives a quick pitch of you and your book, where you see it sitting in the market and why you think the agent or publisher should take a look at it.

- **The first three chapters of the novel.**
  Sometimes there is a stated word count, instead of the three-chapter limit. This is really where the agent or publisher makes their decision. Be-

fore you get too comfortable, assuming they will read all of those chapters, be prepared for the reality. As Madeleine Milburn told me, from the first sentence, agents will be looking for a reason to stop reading. Why? Because they are inundated with submissions every day of the year and the truth is they have a good idea of what they're looking for, even if they can't always fully express what that is. In my experience, it's all about 'voice' – the ethereal term that no one really seems to understand. Basically, it's a tone, an attitude, an assurance that the reader is in safe hands with a writer who knows what they're doing. Of course, that's only the first hurdle. The premise, story and ability to keep the reader turning the page is what will get you that bit closer to a 'yes'. Another agent told me if she's still reading after page one, you are already ahead of about 99% of all the submissions she receives.

One page. Think about that.

- **A synopsis of the book.**
  Synopsis. A word that strikes fear and loathing into the heart of any writer. The idea of having to boil down an 80-100,000-word novel into perhaps 500 words is terrifying. When you first attempt it, you will be convinced it's impossible. In a way, it *is* impossible, but you have to let go of the idea you can put every subplot and

nuance into it. Just hit the main beats. I stopped getting too hung up on the synopsis when an agent told me it's usually the last thing they look at and that their decision has often been made by the time they cast their eyes over it. Unless, of course, the synopsis tells them that your heartwarming romance suddenly develops in to a full-blown intergalactic horror story. That may give them pause.

The waiting game

So, you carefully put all of this together for each of your submissions, researching the agents you should be sending it to and the publishers that accept un-agented submissions. You check off all their bespoke requirements. You have to take notes, write emails and keep track of each one you send out. You agonise over who you will send it to and what you will say in your cover letter (sorry – email!). All of this takes time and lots of effort, but it is nothing in comparison to what awaits once you press send on that last submission. You'll still be surfing a wave of optimism, feeling the warm glow of 'having done something'. You are powerful, in control and ready for the replies to flood your inbox. Sure, there'll be a few *no* sandwiches to swallow, but there's bound to be at least one 'full' request in there, right? If you're yet to enter the shark-infested Sea of Submissions, a 'full' simply means the agent or publisher is sufficiently interested in the sample chapters you sent and now wants to read the whole manuscript.

I was humming with excitement when I sent out my

first batch of *Safe Hands* submissions in 2019. This was an older version of the book and with hindsight, it wasn't ready. I just hadn't realised that yet. By that point I'd been beavering away on the thing, on and off, for the best part of four years but finally I was ready to 'get out there'. I realise that makes me sound like a lonely widower venturing back out onto the dating scene after a twenty-year hiatus, but there are similarities. I was nervous, full of anticipation and ready to sign a prenup – sorry, I mean 'publishing contract'.

"90% of this game is rejection and people telling you no, but that doesn't mean it should stop you. It doesn't mean you're bad or you're never going to get published. It just means the formula wasn't there for that story and that person."

Sarah Leipciger, Episode 144

Back then you could expect to wait anywhere between six to eight weeks to get a response, so after the first few days I stopped refreshing my inbox and tried to forget about it. I wrote some short stories and dared to think about a sequel for *Safe Hands*, all the time realising this would be a fool's errand if no one wanted the first book. Which, surprise-surprise, they didn't. The only good thing was that I had all my rejections within six weeks or thereabouts. At the time I didn't see any positives in this. Six weeks still felt like a long time and then to receive a bunch of form rejection emails – "sorry, whilst the book is well written, it's not for me… blah blah blah" – was pretty grim.

The only personal note I got was from an agent who

represented one of my previous podcast guests. He was a well-known American agent. Perhaps because I'd been referred by one of his clients, he made the time to send me some actual feedback. He liked the writing and the premise but because that version of the book was full of British slang and set in a very English seaside town, he thought it wouldn't have broad appeal outside of the UK. He did, however, say he would be happy for me to send him whatever I decided to write next. I clung to this nugget of positivity, and it got me through another cycle of submissions and rejections, but it was clear this version of the book just wasn't going to cut it.

Even then, I felt like giving up on *Safe Hands*, but couldn't shake the feeling that this was 'the one' that deserved to be published. Perhaps the fact I'd already invested so much time and effort on this book was also a factor. I was like a deluded property investor, pouring money into a house with subsidence. Which is how I came to join Ericka's critique group and embraced the whole 'writing is re-writing' thing. I was ready for round two. Off the book went on yet another submissions odyssey, except this time the days of a six-to-eight-week wait were long gone. After the pandemic, authors could only dream of that kind of timeframe. Replies were taking anywhere between three to six months – if you were lucky enough to even receive a reply. Gird yourself – this seems to be the new norm.

I was in limbo for months at a time. I started writing another novel, but it was hard, always having part of my mind on *Safe Hands* and hoping for that one piece of good news to land in my inbox. I began to wonder not only if I should give up on *Safe Hands*, but maybe I should consider dropping this writing lark altogether. Someone described writing as 'like having homework, every day, for the rest of your life'. Which is a pretty accurate description. Most of the time that's OK, because it's time spent working on something you love, with the promise that one day other people will get to read and enjoy the fruits of your labour. But to work so hard only to leave a book sitting on my hard drive for eternity? What kind of psycho would think that's a good use of time and energy?

> ## "Rejection is really such an important thing to experience as a writer, as it's a process that makes the work more resilient."
>
> Julia Kite, Episode 92

A guiding hand

No. Maybe *Safe Hands* was a pile of crap, after all, and I had zero talent and so what was the point of writing anything else? I would go back to writing the occasional song for my huge Spotify audience (at the time of writing, seven monthly listeners!). I stopped work on the other novel, and was reaching for my guitar, when I spotted a tweet about a new mentorship programme. They were asking for applications and the deadline was imminent. To apply, you had to send the first three chapters of your novel and wait to see if you'd be accepted. What did I have to lose? Before self-doubt could rise up to stop me, I sent the email and chapters and braced myself for the inevitable rejection. I told myself it was the last kick of the ball, an attempt to score a goal in the dying seconds of a football match. If the ref blew time, I would trudge off the field and accept my defeat. It would be time to hang up the boots and retire.

Only a couple of days after applications closed, I received an email. I saw that it was from one of the mentors, Lauren North, who I already knew a little from her appearing on the podcast. *Ah*, I thought, *that's nice of Lauren to send me a personal email to at least let me down gently.*

Wait. What?

I had reached the end of the email and hadn't spotted the rejection. It had to be in there somewhere. I started again from the top, reading the compliments slowly this time, waiting for the other shoe to drop. Except it didn't. There it was in black and white. I had been accepted onto the scheme and Lauren was going to be my mentor! She liked the book, saw lots of promise and already had some ideas of how we could improve the opening chapters. I was over the moon. It might sound like a small thing, but for me, coming when it did, it was huge. So many of us are racked with self-doubt and constantly crave external validation. We long for an objective, knowledgeable peer to tell us we can write. I hadn't realised just how badly I needed that until I received Lauren's email. Thoughts of throwing in the towel now seemed like idle threats. Of course I would never abandon writing. How could I? Cut me open, do I not bleed ink? Such is my fickle nature, I guess.

Lauren is a great writer across multiple genres. She's such a productive, positive person and even before we had our first proper chat, I knew my chances of publication had just gone up exponentially. She told me the book only needed a few tweaks to get it to where it needed to be. This was a big confidence boost and seemed to justify all the re-writing and extra work I had done on it to get it to that point. As with any good mentor, she leads by example, but also looks at the big picture. In addition to helping me add depth, raise the stakes and increase the tension in my novel, she also gave me tips on how to pitch the book and myself. She taught me to adopt a more professional, work-manlike approach to writing and to dare to believe I could be successful.

It is no exaggeration to say that finding a good mentor completely changed my trajectory and outlook. So much so that since my experience with Lauren, I've started to pay it forward and offer mentorship and support to other writers. I get a kick out of seeing them develop their careers, confidence and skillset. Having the right support can make all the difference. I had been knocked down, but wasn't out. With Lauren in my corner, I was back on my feet and ready to fight on.

"Have patience... it's an industry where things take years. Enjoy it and keep going. Don't ever stop."

Lauren North, Episode 135

WRITE HERE, WRITE NOW

1. **Are you thinking of giving up on your dreams of publication?** Maybe you're considering walking away from a book or even writing altogether? STOP.

2. **Get used to hearing the word 'no'.** Remember, it's an acquired taste, but eventually you will gobbling down whole bowls of it and be asking for seconds.

3. **Seek out a champion of your work, or an ally to help you through a difficult patch.** Even if it isn't a formalised mentor/mentee relationship, having another writer to vent your frustrations to can be a huge help. And you can repay the favour by supporting them too.

4. **Revisit the list of reasons you should have pinned to your wall (remember Chapter One?)** Remind yourself what you love about writing. Now make a new list of everything you've achieved along the way, no matter how big or small. Ask yourself – do you really want to quit, when everything could be about to change for the better?

10
Writing as Therapy

Getting through the hard times

> "I didn't realise at the time that I was writing through my process of grief and anger and acceptance, and those kinds of things. After having doubts myself, it was part of my healing process."
>
> Ericka Waller, Episode 151

Writing can be tough. Finding inspiration can be hard, dragging words out of yourself only to feel it's all futile and worthless. Staring at an empty page, and battling to even begin, let alone get to the end of, a draft. And when that first draft is done, there's more work to do. Reading and re-reading, being self-critical, finding the faults and deciding everything you've written is terrible. Then there's the endless cycle of submission, rejection, submission, until it seems like the whole endeavour is pointless.

And that's only the writing side of things. Life is where the real adversity lies and we can under-estimate its impact on our creativity and self-esteem as creatives. In those moments, it's easy to trivialise the power of creativity and the positive effect it can have on our mental health and wellbeing. Let's look at how writing can help you to deal with anything life throws at you, as well as keeping those words flowing.

Write it out

We all have times when writing seems impossible. We feel creatively blocked, or exhausted, out of ideas and energy, convinced we'll never finish another book, story or script. We will often blame these dry spells on lack of time or a busy day job, both of which can put a dent in productivity, but sometimes it goes deeper than that. Whilst I don't really believe in 'writer's block', I do think we can suffer from creative burnout. It's akin to the golfer trying too hard to hit the ball (again with the golf analogies, Wayne?). Ask any golf coach and they will tell you the more relaxed and loose you are, the more likely you are to strike the ball cleanly and hit a great shot. I think it's the same with writing. Sometimes we're so focused on reaching an arbitrary word count, or grinding out a half-baked scene, that we seize up, lose our mojo and the joy of creativity.

Alongside that, there are times when our lives outside of writing obviously have to take precedence. Health issues, relationship problems, grief, finances, work and all the other stuff that most of us hate to deal with. It's often why we like to write fiction; it's the one place we have complete control over events. Well, unless our characters derail things.

Whether creative or life issues, writing is a great tool to help us find our way through difficulty. Many of the guests I've spoken to on *The Write Place* agree.

"It was actually a mental breakdown that got me into writing. And at that point, when life was about as low as it can get, I turned to writing."

CJ Walley, Screenwriter, Episode 82

When we hit a bump in the road – either on the page or out in the real world – it's tempting to stop writing altogether. I've found the opposite. Double down. Write more, but accept it may not be on your work-in-progress. This is why many people find keeping a journal or diary can help them process problems, putting down on paper how they feel at any given time. At various points in my life, I've given it a go, but having a formal structure like this doesn't work for me. The diary format makes me feel like I should be specifically writing about my day and structuring my thoughts accordingly. I also feel guilty if I miss a day. If it's an uneventful day, I find myself scrabbling around for something interesting that might have happened. I've even been tempted to make something up. Which is ridiculous.

Whilst a diary isn't my cup of tea, it may well scratch that itch for you. So give it a try. If, however, you've already tried it and not found it useful, you should consider Morning Pages. I first heard about Morning Pages from a friend, who recommended I read Julia Cameron's book, *The Artist's Way*. One of the suggested techniques Julia puts forward is the idea of freewriting a set amount of pages every day. As the name suggests, the morning is considered a good time to do this, but I think whenever you can fit it in is fine too. My version differs slightly from Julia's, and you should definitely read *The Artist's Way*, but it's the method I've developed for myself over the years.

It's not something I religiously do every day of my life. It's a crutch I lean on in times of need. That might be when I'm feeling creatively fried, or when life bears down on me to such an extent that writing, or any creative endeavour seems impossible. With all the rejection that comes with the territory of being a writer, it's been invaluable in pushing me through the pain barrier to keep going. Here's how I do it, and why it works for me.

They're only words

I have an A5-sized notebook – I suppose what would be considered a normal diary size. The rule is I must fill at least two pages with words. Notice I say 'words', not 'writing'. This takes away some of the pressure. For you it might be three or four pages, or if you prefer, set a minimum time.

It may take a few days to find what works best. The idea is to write, freely, without too much thought and with no constraints on content, form, cohesion or anything else. Just write. When you first try it, you may even begin with something like, 'I have no idea what I'm going to write. I don't have anything to say. In fact, I'm starting to wonder why I'm doing this…' and on and on it goes. What you will find, in a very short space of time, is that 'real' stuff starts to come out. Your thoughts, feelings, fears, anxieties. You may want to vent about a work colleague, or something that happened at home. You may even end up writing about your WIP, or an issue you're having with a character or plot thread. Whatever. It doesn't matter. It can be total drivel, but the idea is to come to the page with no expectations or plan. Put pen to paper and write. It's like sucking out the poison so you can heal enough to find your way back to whatever you've been working on, or would like to be working on.

> **"I was having treatment for post-traumatic stress disorder. I was undergoing counselling, and this counsellor decided she was going to try a writing therapy with me, because she discovered that during normal talking sessions, I would really struggle to express myself. Quite often I would be overwhelmed by emotion."**
>
> Matt Johnson, Episode 62

It's exactly the same process as you would likely adopt if you were seeing a therapist. You talk and they listen. Often, you are asked to talk about the first thing that comes to mind and to take it from there. With this daily writing routine, the page is your therapist. You will be amazed at how quickly you'll see the positive effects. We are writers, used to organising and communicating complicated ideas and emotions. Getting down our own thoughts helps us to make sense of the world and create a narrative that lets us navigate our challenges. But even if you don't want to commit to a daily routine, there's nothing stopping you from writing about an episode or specific area of your life to make sense of things.

If all that sounds a bit too reflective and spiritual for you, there are still other ways writing can calm your mind and ease self-doubt or creative blocks. If I'm stuck on a novel and really can't break the deadlock or find the motivation to push through the uncertainty, I find simple flash fiction exercises can help. For the uninitiated, flash fiction is simply very short fiction – anything from 50-200 words. When I was a member of Phoenix Writers, we were given a simple writing prompt and a strict word count to write something that had a beginning, middle and end. You must be strict with the word count. If the target is 100 words, then the piece must be exactly 100 words. It's a great way to practise editing, but it also forces you to be creative and loose. The wilder the writing prompt, the better. If you want to really lean into the freewriting aspect of it, give yourself a strict time limit too. That way, you'll have to write whatever comes to mind. There's no time to over-think your issues, it's fun and takes you away from the pressure of your work-in-progress. I'll give you some prompts at the end of the chapter.

For many of us, aspects of our real selves, families or life experiences, often find their way into our work – whether we're aware of it or not – but writing directly about life events can also have practical uses. I discovered this through personal experience, when I had unexpected health issues a few years ago.

Solving a mystery

One day, after a long bike ride, I was sitting in the garden, cooling down and chatting to my daughter. Halfway through a sentence I stopped and asked her, "Hang on. Have I literally just told you this? Am I repeating myself?"

It was the most intense feeling of déjà vu I had ever experienced, and moments later I had the first of what would be six 'episodes' that day. I felt my head being pulled back and I blacked out for several seconds. I came round, still sat in the chair, to see my daughter's terrified face. I felt the same terror and disorientation. I went to hospital and continued to collapse throughout the day. I was frightened and unable to work out what had happened. At the time, the doctors were short of answers and were suggesting there could be a problem with my heart.

The very next day, whilst still in hospital, I grabbed my laptop and wrote, in as much detail as possible, about what had happened to me. I wanted to get it down whilst it was still fresh in my mind, before I could romanticise it, or add the poetic licence we writers of fiction are often prone to. I tried to be as honest and factual as possible. Strangely, it made me feel better. I saved it and put it away.

Over the next couple of months, I had lots of tests and a cardio MRI scan and was then given a completely clean bill of health. I was told, "Oh, you're just the kid who used to faint in assembly." (a direct quote!). So I accepted it as 'one of those things' and got on with my life. Until three years later when I was working at an event, sitting with my edit suite at the back of a conference room, when that same sense of déjà vu hit me and the next thing I knew, the house lights were on and I was lying on my back with a couple of hundred people staring at me, asking if I was OK. This time I was referred to a neurologist. I thought about when it had happened years before and remembered I'd written an account of my experiences. When I saw the neurologist, I was able to share key aspects of it with him, and he quickly suspected the likely cause. I was sent for more tests and eventually diagnosed with focal epilepsy.

In the immediate aftermath of those initial seizures (as I now know they were), my natural response was to write about it. At the time, this was to help me process what had happened, but it went on to serve a very real practical use in helping diagnose the issue. And in the days after my diagnosis, when I felt shocked and depressed, I wrote a song, which also helped me put things into perspective. Things weren't as bad as they seemed, there is medication to help and I'm lucky enough to have an incredibly supportive wife and family. But writing helped me – and continues to help me – through adversity. Whether it's life, or problems on the page, I'm living proof that words can pull you through.

> **"I had bereavement therapy, which was life-changing. But it also really changed my writing because it fed into the story and this theme of trapped grief. I think it gave it an authenticity that hadn't been there before."**
>
> Clare Empson, Episode 112

WRITE HERE, WRITE NOW

1. **Try Morning Pages, or your version of it.** Even if it's just fifteen minutes a day, try freewriting, allowing yourself to write for the sake of writing.

2. **If journalling is more your thing, start a diary or journal, but don't be too hard on yourself if you can't sustain it over a long period.**

3. **Try some flash fiction.** Here are two prompts to get you started.

   - Write 100 words that include the phrase 'never tasted so good'.

   - Write 150 words on the theme of jealousy.

11

Why I Eventually Chose Self-Publishing

And why I think you
should consider it too

> "I think more and more authors are finding the support is just not there in the traditional model. I see everyone working at publishers, they're all overworked and they just don't have the budget or the time or the bandwidth."
>
> Stefan Mohamed, Episode 249

When you begin to take writing seriously, working towards publication, it seems there really is only one way of doing it. The 'proper' way. You know, get an agent and score a publishing deal with one of the 'big five' publishing companies. Pull down that fat advance, quit your day job and start cranking out those novels for your adoring readers, baby. If you can't achieve success that way, you're not a real writer. At least that's what I, and many others believed for a long time. But the industry has changed – and continues to do so. We need to change our attitudes with it. In this chapter, we'll look at the other options out there and why 'traditional' publishing might not be all it's cracked up to be.

Coming to a crossroads

Through years of honing, gaining support and validation from other writers and with the help of a good mentor, I knew I now had a book that deserved to be read. I saw it as for crime fans who were looking for something different to the usual police procedural or Jack Reacher-style thrillers that tend to dominate the market. What I hadn't considered is that by taking a step away from the tried-and-tested genre tropes, I was making the book harder to sell to traditional publishers.

On Lauren's suggestion, in addition to my submission to large traditional publishers and agents, I also started to try some of the newer 'digital-first' publishers. Companies like Bookouture, Boldwood and The Book People (other companies that don't begin with the letter B are available). At the time of writing, these are all relatively new kids on the block and, as the name suggests, they initially focus on the digital sales of the book. Often run by ex-traditional publishing figures, these publishers are nimble, know the genre markets very well and specialise in reaching an online community of readers. They don't rely on doing huge print runs and sticking to rigid publication schedules. One of the major frustrations for traditionally published authors is that it can often be eighteen months, to two years between book releases. But with digital-first publishers, if a book is ready to launch – they put it out.

Digital-first publishers often have a slick online process and many of them accept unsolicited submissions. In other words, you don't have to have an agent. They also give you a response in a much shorter space of time. Now I was getting my rejections in a matter of weeks, not months. A no is still a no, but at least I wasn't left in limbo for half a year at a time. Despite the rejections, I was starting to get closer to a yes. A couple of the publishers asked to read the full manuscript and gave me encouraging feedback. The consensus seemed to be they liked it but weren't quite sure how it fitted with their other books. They wanted to be able to slot it into a clear category and established genre, but the fact it was a crime novel told from the perspective of a criminal made it more unusual. I thought this was a good thing, but as with most mainstream businesses, I understand it's easier for publishers to sell something that fits into a neat little pigeonhole.

One publisher in particular seemed very interested. The woman who was reading the book kept me up to date with her progress. She continued to tell me she was enjoying it. She asked me what plans I had for potential sequels. I began to feel my hopes rising again, but I was also coming to the end of my patience. I was hardened to rejection now and, despite the promising signs, I was half-expecting another bowl of 'no'. I told Lauren that if the book hadn't been picked up by a certain date, I was going to bite the bullet and self-publish. Months and years of my life were disappearing, and I was sick of waiting for some stranger to tell me they would put out my book. There were other factors at play too.

The power of validation

Only a few years ago, I would have seen this as an admission of failure. Self-publishing – before it was rebranded to the sexier-sounding 'Indie Publishing' – was seen as vanity publishing. *Your book isn't good enough to be published by a 'real' publisher, so you do it independently and call yourself an author.* The truth is indie authors have been releasing professional, well-written and edited books for a long time now, but it's only relatively recently that it's become more accepted in the writing community. I say, 'the writing community', because what you soon realise is that readers couldn't care less how your book is published – and never have been. If it looks professional and keeps them gripped from the first page to the last, then as far as they're concerned, it's a *real book*.

> **"I'm an independent author, so I choose
> when I publish. And so for me, it's much
> more of a clean process. I finish my draft,
> I do my own edit and then it goes to my
> story editor. I make my changes, it goes to a
> proofreader. I make my changes, I publish."**
>
> Joanna Penn, Episode 65

The snobbery and reticence has tended to come from some successful traditionally published authors and, of course, the big publishers themselves. The latter is understandable. Their entire business model is being threatened. And to a certain extent, I do understand why many authors would have reservations. Without the external validation of an agent or publishing gatekeeper isn't there a danger that standards will slip and lots of terrible books will appear? Yes. That is a real concern and, especially in the early years of Amazon's CreateSpace publishing platform, lots of amateurish efforts were unleashed into the wild. Awful covers and badly written books that weren't proofread, let alone edited. Unreadable books that looked homemade and only reinforced the idea that self-published books were crap. Even now, if you look hard enough, you can still find those books on Amazon, but the market decides what's successful and what's not. And after all, there are lots of traditionally published books that have some, or all, of the same flaws. When it comes down to it, there are only two kinds of books: good books and bad books.

Having created and hosted a writing podcast for over a decade, I've seen the attitudes of writers soften, reflecting how the industry itself has changed. Many traditionally published authors have told me, off-air, they're unhappy with their traditional publisher. The lack of control. Having no input on the cover, the release schedule and, often, even the title of their own book, can be frustrating.

> **"I have dipped my toe in the traditional publishing world a couple of times and gone, 'The water's a bit cold, I'm getting out'... but I'd never say never."**
>
> Angela C Nurse, Episode 224

Judgement day

So the day came when I finally got the rejection I had suspected was coming. The person who'd read my book had enjoyed it. She even admitted she was *surprised* how much she liked it – a back-handed compliment, if ever there was one. But when she had taken it to the rest of the team, no one was quite sure where they would place it. So they passed on it.

I know this is going to sound like total BS – like the

type of thing you say when you've been dumped by someone you love – but by the time it happened, I was secretly glad about it. *Yeah, yeah. Sure you were, Wayne. If Sexy Trad came crawling back, you'd be there before you could say 'lack of self-respect'.*

Moving along…

Between the time I had told Lauren of my plans and getting that rejection, I had started to do some real research about the nuts and bolts of putting out a book yourself. I was determined the book had to be as indistinguishable from a mass-market paperback as possible, which meant investing my time (and money) into the venture. If you choose this route, it's important to consider it as an investment. An investment in yourself, your passion for writing and your long-term publishing goals. I had some non-negotiables:

The book had to be edited, copy edited and proofread before release.

The cover had to be slick and professional and – just as importantly – it had to be right for the genre.

On that latter point, people really do judge a book by its cover. Within a couple of seconds, they need to know if the book is crime, sci-fi, romance, horror, literary fiction… or whatever genre you're aiming for. I attend so many book fairs and events where self-published authors have skimped on this area and as a consequence, their covers either look amateurish or give no indication as to their genre. Researching other similar books is essential before you even begin to design a cover or brief a designer. I already had some design experience, so I was keen to have a go at doing my own cover. The caveat was that if it didn't pass muster,

I would commission someone else to do it.

With the editing of the book, I'd already had lots of structural edits from established writers and a final polish from Lauren, so I knew the book was in good shape from a story and structure perspective. However, for the copy edit and proofread, I employed a professional for the job. Debra Newhouse has worked on both my novels so far – *Safe Hands* and the sequel *The Call Back* – as well as the book you're reading now. She's a pleasure to work with. It's not simply a case of spotting typos and punctuation errors. Just as a traditional publisher would, a good copy editor uses an established style guide to give the manuscript consistency in formatting. For example, ensuring speech marks are the same throughout or standardising things like mobile phone text conversations, or the way numbers and times are written. Aspects most writers wouldn't even consider when drafting or editing their manuscript. Debra's work elevated my manuscript to a professional level and made me confident I was sending out a polished book. It was the one area I was happy to leave to a pro. Everything else? I jumped in and sucked up as much information as I could.

An exciting learning curve

There are many, many technicalities to grasp, skills to learn and hoops to jump through on the way to publishing your own book. At first, I was intimidated but it quickly became exhilarating. I hadn't learned so many new things since I had begun my career in video production almost twenty years before. Typesetting, layout, marketing, ISBNs, PR, KDP, print-on-demand… the list goes on and on. I say this not to put you off, but to give you a sense of the size of the task and to make you appreciate it's not just a case of throwing your manuscript up onto Amazon, with a cover you made on your phone. You don't have to get hands-on with every single aspect, but bear in mind the less you're willing to learn for yourself, the more of your hard-earned cash you're going to need to invest.

> **"I kind of push back against the term self-publishing, because you don't do this on your own. You have a team around you, but once the writing is done, it's your job to manage that team."**
>
> Rachel Amphlett, Episode 64

You can even hand everything over to a company or individual to take care of everything for you. For example, with my imprint, Pick Lock Publishing, I now help other authors get their books out into the world, taking care of all the technical stuff - cover design, typesetting and uploading the finished files to the various sales platforms for them to manage. This means they have complete control and get to keep all of their royalties. They only pay me for the production side of things.

For authors with bigger budgets looking for a completely hands-off experience, there are 'partner' or 'hybrid' publishers (vanity publishers in everything but name) who will charge you to produce the book AND still take a cut of your royalties. They can also charge a fortune for printing. Yes, I'm biased, but that particular business model does irritate me. It costs thousands and the author still doesn't have control or receive their full royalties.

But initially, I would encourage you to at least look into it a little more and see if you think it's right for you. I know many of you still dream of seeing your book in a high street bookshop or winning a top prize. An indie book is highly unlikely to end up on a shelf in Waterstones (or Barnes & Noble for my American readers), and you won't be eligible for many of the prestigious literary awards, but you can still distribute through all online book stores and, of course, Amazon. All the big book retailers can still order your book if a reader requests it. Most readers buy their books online and many traditionally published authors still don't find shelf space in major book shop chains. Competition is fierce.

Perhaps you think being traditionally published will mean your publisher takes care of all that pesky marketing and social media. WRONG. You will still be expected to 'build your platform', arrange your own book tours and find places to promote your book. My view is if I'm going to have to do that anyway, I may as well do it for myself, while retaining the royalties and control of my book.

But everyone is different and I understand we all have different motivations to write and publish our work. You must find the right way for you. All I would urge is that you at least consider indie publishing as an alternative.

As for me, *Safe Hands* was released in November 2023, with its sequel *The Call Back*, following in January 2025. I hope to complete the trilogy in 2026. But what *will* I do if Sexy Trad does walk back into my life? Well… I guess it depends on what she's offering.

"Indie is coming like a freight train.
We're getting higher royalties and indie
authors are really changing the industry,
in a way that it probably needs
to be changed."

Rebecca Thorne, Episode 252

"Now that I've done it, I'm like, this is
amazing. I don't want to ever stop doing
indie. Regardless of whether I continue
with traditional as well, I enjoy
being a hybrid author."

Melissa Sercia, Episode 159

WRITE HERE, WRITE NOW

1. **If you're yet to be published, ask yourself what it is about the traditional model that appeals to you.** Is it because you want to see your book in Waterstones? You want to be eligible for respected industry awards?

2. **If you are already traditionally published, and becoming disillusioned, consider why you're frustrated.** Is it the lack of control? The long gaps between publication? Or something else? Might indie publishing be the answer?

3. **Do an audit of your current skills and experience.** What can you already bring to the process and where are the gaps? Are you willing to learn?

4. **Take some time to research indie publishing.** Check out *The Creative Penn Podcast, The Write Place* or *The Bestseller Experiment*. Even if you're a technophobe or don't think you have the skills and patience to do it, there's lots of support out there. I offer courses, help and advice at my website wkwproductions.co.uk or take a look at the Alliance of Independent Authors website for more hints and tips.

12
From Pod to Page

Lessons from a
decade of interviews

> "Write to be remembered."
>
> Dan Howarth, Episode 155

Ever wondered why and how podcasts come into existence? In this chapter, I'll give you a behind-the-scenes look at *The Write Place* and tell you what I've learned speaking to hundreds of guests over more than a decade.

It's been a long road

When my then co-host, Leah, and I started the first incarnation of *The Write Place – The Joined Up Writing Podcast –* we weren't really sure what we were doing or how the show would evolve. It was 2014 and, believe it or not, podcasts were still relatively niche back then. This was before every celebrity and their dog (literally!) had a podcast. Lots of people weren't even sure how to listen to podcasts.

This meant the stakes were low and we could find our feet. We began with just the two of us, chatting about writing – our writing, technique, the issues faced by writers and anything else writing-related. That was fun, but we knew we weren't going to be able to sustain a show on nothing more than two unknown writers babbling on. We would need guests.

Aside from the practical aspect of creating show content, it would also give us an excuse to approach authors, get their backstory, ask their advice and find inspiration for us and other writers. We started off with people we personally knew and cast the net wider as we went. Leah left early in the show's history, but I eventually established a loose structure for my interviews, which is more or less still intact more than ten years on from that first episode.

I always begin by encouraging the guest to talk about and promote their latest project, delving into the themes and motivations for the work and giving them a chance to sell it to my listeners. Then we step back in time, to the guest's earliest memories of writing and work forward from there. We discover their path to publication, hear about their process, what they've learned along the way and how they've handled the difficult periods. I ask them to share their favourite piece of writing or creative advice, and we finish by looking forward to whatever they have coming up in the future.

"You can be good, you can be good to work with, and you can be on time. Unless you are phenomenally good, you need to be at least two of these three things. If it's your occupation, your profession, then you have to behave in a professional way."

Natasha Calder, Episode 188

Over the years, there have been new additions and changes to the format – 'The Book That Saved Your Life' and 'Their Darkest Hour', being two of the latest – but in the main, my intention has always been to have real conversations with real writers and to go with the flow as much as possible. Some chats have been funny, some have been inspirational or thought-provoking and, very occasionally, some have been hard work! But through the show I have met and become friends with writers who have stayed in my support network many years after we first met on the podcast. Aside from the friendships, I've also picked up help and advice that has changed my writing life and played a huge part in my journey to publication.

"Take creative risks. Continually push yourself out of safe harbour. That's where the growth happens."

Margaret Douaihy, Episode 183

If you've come this far, hopefully I've imparted some of that knowledge but to round things off, I wanted to bring it all together into what I see as being the sum of all those conversations. It was the driving force and central idea behind this book: PERSEVERANCE.

Before I began talking to other – more successful and experienced – writers, I really did think they would be able to give me 'the secret'. One killer piece of advice, maybe a lesser-known bit of writing craft or a hidden back door into the industry. I delved into their childhoods and probed their CV. I asked where they write, when they write, how they write. Which always led to the now clichéd favourite – are you a pantser or a planner? I even asked *why* they write. I still ask all of these questions, and more, by the way. The difference is that now I'm not expecting any of their answers to be THE answer to the puzzle that seems to be 'making it as a writer'. The meaning of which, is different for all of us. Maybe you just want to have an article or story published in a magazine? Or something in an anthology? You might have aspirations to be a novelist or a screenwriter. Maybe even a poet (my condolences). But as I made clear way back in Chapter Two, if you write, then you're a writer.

In terms of 'making it'? There's only one difference between you and any of the writers you consider to be where you aspire to be. Yes, there's an element of talent, but as the years and interviews have rolled on, I've come to realise talent really isn't all it's cracked up to be. Sure, it helps. We all want to be good at what we do. It's why we learn the craft and read books and seek out writing podcasts to devour. If you take the time to try the exercises and tips I've given you throughout the book, you will develop and gain confidence, or find ways to make it through when writing is difficult. You will keep getting better at what you do. So, if you're willing to treat everything you write as a learning experience, and you seek good critique from other writers, the talent will take care of itself.

"It never gets easier. People ask, 'By book two or three does it get easier?' but it doesn't, because you make it hard by challenging yourself."

C.J. Tudor, Episode 101

But no. It's not the talent. Neither is it about the 'lucky breaks' some writers seem to have. As the saying goes, 'If your ship comes in, you have to be able to row out to meet it.' In other words, you still have to be standing on the dock and have the strength and will to take that last journey. There is only a single difference between you and the writer who has achieved their goal:

THEY KEPT GOING.

That's it. There is no magic wand or special incantation. They simply hung on in there until something happened for them. That might be finding their dream agent, landing a publishing deal or just finishing a book good enough to publish themselves. If you keep putting one foot – or word – in front of another you WILL get there.

Best-selling author, Laura Pearson, is a great example of this. Her story sums up what it means to be a real writer. Here's just an excerpt of her story.

"I wrote a book… it had taken me forever and I got an agent. It needed a lot of work, and when I told her about my idea for my second book… she much preferred that one. I wrote it over the next couple of years, then it went out on submission… and didn't sell. Then I lost my agent because she left agenting… and that was just a real knock. But behind every overnight success story, I think there's at least ten years of hard work and rejection."

Best-selling author, Laura Pearson, Episode 212

Many of us would have given up after that first roadblock. Laura shook it off, pushed on and kept writing. That meant when she finally did find the right home for her book, she had a bunch of other novels already written and available for submission. At the time of writing, Laura has now had multiple bestsellers and has found a growing audience who loves what she does. Imagine if she had given up after that first, second or third setback? What might (not) have been? Laura's story of rejection is not unusual, but her reaction to it is rare. So many of us quit when success is just around the corner. Even if it isn't 'just around the corner', we should write as if it's only moments away. Be ready to row out and meet that ship.

"I wrote another book that I shelved and then another book that I finished, but I got rejected on that 98 times."

Bonnie Garmus, Episode 168

98 times – and Bonnie wasn't exaggerating! So pick up that pen, open your laptop or do whatever it is you do when it's time to get the words down. Laugh in the face of adversity and write, write, write.

WRITE HERE, WRITE NOW

1. **Go to www.realwritersneverquit.com (or scan the QR code below) to download the 'Real Writers Never Quit' poster, print it out and stick it above your writing space, next to the 'Why I Write' list you should already have pinned up there.** There's also a desktop wallpaper version and some other free goodies, when you sign up to my Write Here, Write Now newsletter. Anytime you're even considering giving up what you love, give your head a wobble and get back to work.

2. **Then, anytime you're looking for an extra shot of inspiration or advice, dip into the final chapter where you'll find even more quotes and titbits from my legion of guests.** I, and every one of the writers I've had the pleasure to meet, is rooting for you. Don't let us down. Do what you were born to do, because real writers never quit.

13
The Well of Inspiration

Your next chapter

> "It just sets my imagination on fire, you know?'
>
> Elena Passarello, Episode 114

What follows is a selection of quotes from more than a decade of episodes of *The Joined Up Writing Podcast* and *The Write Place*. I've grouped them into broad themes to create a well of inspiration you can dip into any time you need that little extra boost.

On why writers write

Most writers don't start because they have a plan or a career goal. They start because something pulls at them, nags them and won't quite leave them alone. These voices speak to that early urge, the private reasons people return to writing long before anyone is watching.

> **"There's a quote I love about running – 'Nothing has ever broken my heart like running, and yet I can't breathe without it.' And I honestly feel like that about writing. I have to do it."**
>
> Jackie Kabler, Episode 128

"I love the idea. I love the craft of it. You know,
I really love words. I've wanted to put out stories
that other people would enjoy reading and now
I've done that, I'm getting reviews back and, you
know, it just makes you get all weepy inside."

Julia Boggio, Episode 180

"Around second grade, my parents got divorced.
And then I wrote a story about a little boy whose
mom died, and my teacher and my mom both
started crying. And I didn't even realise in my
own eight-year-old psyche that that's how I was
processing my parents' divorce. I don't know
if I was any good at it – certainly not at eight
years old – but I think it was definitely a skill
I had to learn. I wanted to express myself."

Joey Hartstone, Episode 175

"I actually want to write the story; the stories
need to be written. And I want to put them out
there. That's all. That's good enough for me."

A.D. Barker, Episode 157

"I never had the confidence, actually, to think, oh, I could write. It was something I did right from an early age, but I never thought of writing because, academically, I was always pushed towards the sciences and maths and that area. But I was always writing. Always in the background. It was a way of getting through life. And in the process of putting pen to paper, I decided that I actually wanted to give voice to the community that I grew up in."

Rosanna Amaka, Episode 119

"When I was probably about six in school, there was this thing once a week where the teacher got us to volunteer to just tell a story to the class and I loved that. But then they started getting us to try to write them down and there everything went wrong, because of my dyslexia. It was way later, when I'd learned to type, that I found that, amazingly, I could write and I was hooked."

Rod Duncan, Episode 120

"I think I'm still learning that myself, actually. The writing, I think, is where it begins and structuring a story so that it can move someone else and hopefully move them in a meaningful way is very fulfilling to me and I think that's why I do it. I think I sit down, and if I can tell a story worth telling and empathetically move someone through that story, then I think I've done my job."

David Wappel, Episode 117

"Aside from just the simple fact of, you know, getting lost in writing, whether it's on a notebook or on the screen, I really love storytelling… I have such a huge imagination, a very vivid imagination, and I love creating characters and worlds and just making them come to life."

Melissa Sercia, Episode 159

"When I was seven or eight, my mother challenged me to write a story on my own… The narrative was all over the place, it had no plot, but I remember the look on my mother's face when she finished reading it and it was just this sort of disbelief. She kept asking me if I came up with this by myself, all on my own. The look on her face is, sort of, this high that I've been chasing ever since."

S.A. Cosby, Episode 204

"I began as an actor in my early twenties, did all the usual things as a young actor. Touring, couple of stints in the West End. And then, like many actors, I think I started to realise that instead of waiting for the phone to ring, it was far more fruitful to sit down and write your own material."

Julian Dutton, Episode 124

"I love reading so much and there are so many books that mean a lot to me and have impacted my life. You know, even if they're very entertaining or funny or flighty, sometimes that really can impact my life in a way. And I want to be able to do that for other people."

Becky Robison, Episode 152

"For me as a writer, the entire process is so intricately connected. I mean, I am both at my happiest and my most miserable when I'm writing, you know? I got addicted to this very early on and I can't quit it yet. It's a monkey on my back. A compulsion."

Jessica Anthony, Episode 125

"There's a kind of magic to storytelling.
Whether that's on film or, you know, in fiction
or whatever it is, where you can transport
somebody else to somewhere else… and make
them actually feel things almost as viscerally
as if it's happening to them in person."

Paul Howarth, Episode 160

"That's what my books are all about. It's about the food that we put on the table for the ones we love. And that's at the heart of all my books."

Jo Thomas, Episode 140

On writing craft

At some point, instinct meets intention. Writing stops being just something we feel our way through and starts becoming something we pay attention to. These quotes explore the small, often invisible decisions writers make about language, structure, and how a story lands with a reader.

"I'm quite interested in rhythm at sentence level, and then at paragraph level. If the rhythm is wrong, the whole thing feels off."

Susanna Dickey, Episode 132

"I'm always asking 'What does this scene do?' If it doesn't do anything, it probably shouldn't be there."

Paul Howarth, Episode 79

"I try to make sure every character wants something. Even if they don't say it, the want is there and it drives the page."

Gail Aldwin, Episode 193

"I would say trust your reader and use more white space. You know, don't over-explain things. And particularly in a psychological thriller, you want to unsettle your reader. So you don't want to be too sort of sledgehammer-y with the scary bits. You just want to drop in a couple of slightly chilling, unsettling thoughts every so often. Something that's going to intrigue the reader."

Lesley Kara, Episode 255

"I'm a big believer in specificity. If you choose the right detail, it does the emotional work for you."

Maram Taibah, Episode 127

"I'm always thinking about the reader experience. Where are they leaning in, where are they confused, where are they bored."

Leona Deakin, Episode 139

"It's a thriller. You have to earn the pace. You can't just sprint for two hundred pages and hope it works."

Steve Cavanagh, Episode 122

"I'm always thinking about what the reader knows and what they don't know. That's where suspense is."

C.J. Tudor, Episode 77

"I like to find the emotional spine of the story. Once I know what the story is actually about, the scenes make more sense."

Clare Beams, Episode 149

"I don't think I could write about something
that I wasn't completely obsessed with. I need
to feel like I'm sort of in love with the thing,
or the person, or the moment that I'm trying
to write about. Otherwise I just don't think
I would have the stamina to stay with it."

Elena Passarello, Episode 114

"I think voice is everything.
When you hear a voice on the page and
you feel like you know that person,
you will follow them anywhere."

Merle Nyegate, Episode 219

"Everything I know about writing is like:
How is this scene – even the most casual,
comic relief, or character beat scene – taking
us in some way toward the conclusion,
toward the culmination of the themes?"

Mac Rogers, Episode 97

"Writing... feels like I'm not wasting
anything. You can use your memories
from ten years ago or some thought you
had the other day or something you've
seen on a street... it all can show up."

Jumon Malouf, Episode 80

"Robert McKee says you should write the truth, and I think that's where everybody's voice is. Be completely honest about what it is to be human, what it is for your character to be human, what it is you think about the world and how you observe it, and just be truthful."

Senta Rich, Episode 186

"Facts aren't stories and stories aren't facts. So just because you've got a ton of facts doesn't mean you've got a story. It's about how you frame your story in a way that makes it interesting and relevant for other people."

Melanie McGrath, Episode 90

"Start reading your own work back. And I mean, I always tell people not to wince because it doesn't matter when it's not good, but you'll know when it's good. You know when it gets better. So that's the key thing – to keep going until it gets good because you can't worry about the bad stuff. But I did keep copies just to remind myself of this. You know, don't get too big for your boots, mate. Go back and look at your early work."

Christopher Fowler, Episode 133

"Come in late, get out early. You need to start as late as possible. In the first paragraph, we need to know who it's about, what they want, and perhaps why they want it and where they are. You know, do that in the opening. We don't need a lovely flowery passage… Nearly every story I've written, I've got rid of the first half page."

Bead Roberts, Episode 53

"It's about being as outrageous as you dare with your material. I think it's that business of always daring yourself with your writing. Have you really pushed this as far as you can? Much of my time as a teacher is daring the students to pursue their material even further, even to a point where they don't necessarily feel comfortable, so that it starts to open and change its possibilities."

Edward Carey, Episode 227

"My books need to have my DNA in them. And I think as long as you can put your own stamp on the work, people will connect to it."

S.J. Watson, Episode 166

"There's a tool called 'The Five Whys'. It's used in change management to understand root cause analysis. So quite often when I'm plotting, I will go, 'OK, so you might know who the murderer is, but why have they done that?' I keep asking why. I think, particularly in thrillers, understanding that motivation is really, really helpful."

Sarah Bonner, Episode 163

"The real magic is that your characters come alive and speak to you. If you're really succeeding, they're telling you what they're thinking, what they want to do and they give you their dialogue, if they're powerful enough."

Sean Lusk, Episode 171

"There are some sort of theatrics involved, you know, where I would only write by candlelight, for example. So the blinds would be drawn, because it doesn't make any sense for me to be looking out the window and seeing cars driving past when I'm trying to write about Victorian London. Not to sound too Daniel Day-Lewis about it, but there are little tricks."

Paddy Crewe, Episode 169

"Eat dessert first... write the scene that you are excite about first. Don't chain yourself to writing everything sequentially."

Hanna Jameson, Episode 98

On Revising and Getting a Fresh Perspective

Very few writers get it right first time. For most of us, clarity comes later, through distance, patience, and a willingness to look again. This section is about that shift, from protecting the work to shaping it into something stronger.

"I used to think that writing a book was writing a book, and now I realise that writing a book really is editing the book."

Kate Harrison, Episode 123

"By looking at how information is revealed, I can see... Am I repeating myself too many times or not enough?"

Karin Salvalaggio, Episode 95

"Is a scene or a chapter or a few chapters
are moving the central plot forward? If the
answer is no, then probably take them out."

Clio Cornish, Episode 89

"Editing isn't tearing stories apart. A good editor takes the story that's there and makes it clearer."

Liam J. Cross, Episode 93

"One of my favourite parts of the whole process
is, once I've written the first draft, I write all
of the chapters on Post-it notes – just a quick
summary of what is in each chapter – and
then I lay them out on my kitchen table and I
stand back and think does the story flow, do I
need to move these chapters around to build
suspense? There're a few friends I have that
aspire to writing. They put too much pressure
on themselves to write that perfect first hundred
pages. And so, I think what I've learned is it
doesn't matter if your first draft, or three or four
drafts, are not good enough, because you can
work with it and hone it and move it around."

Leona Deakin, Episode 139

"What I always tell my authors is that when we're editing, please leave your ego at the door because there's no point in getting defensive over every suggestion that your editor gives you. The editor is trying to make the book the best it can be. I think as a writer, we're a little bit too close to our own work and we don't necessarily see it how the reader is going to see it. The editor's job is to be that first reader and to mediate between writer and reader so that what's actually on the page is what the author intended."

Louise Walters, Episode 138

"I actually really enjoy the editing. The first draft is always fast. I try to do that within about twelve weeks just because I feel that if I don't, I lose that sense of urgency in the story. So in the second draft, I actually I use an analogy. It's almost like your first draft is a sketch and we need to go back and start editing that… colouring it in."

Rachel Amphlett, Episode 64

"It becomes, you know, just something I cannot leave alone. People often ask me, 'How do you know to stop editing?' And I know to stop editing when I can read the entire thing through and not mind any of it."

Roz Morris, Episode 106

"Before uni I was very much a proponent of the
first draft being this kind of holy object, where
the creative spark is, and I couldn't possibly
compromise it or dilute it in any way. But
learning the importance of honing and crafting,
and getting your story or poem or book into
the best possible shape, was really valuable."

Stefan Mohamed, Episode 249

On process, planning and finding your own way

There's a lot of noise around how writing is supposed to
be done. Plot it all out. Don't plot at all. Write every day.
Wait for the right moment. These voices cut through that
by showing how different writers actually find their way
in, often by trial, error, and quiet persistence. As I've said
before… if it works for you, it's the right way.

"I write a lot like I walk and drive. I get lost
a lot. It takes me to some really interesting
places and sometimes the place I go via is more
interesting than where I'm going to. So it can
have some real advantages, but it means it's slow."

Emma Viskic, Episode 86

"I'm a *planter*, which is a kind of in the middle between the one who plans and the one who just hits the ground running… I have a beginning, I have an end, I have a couple of key scenes I know I want to include. The rest, I'm just letting it tell itself to me as I write, because I just feel if I planned it any more than that, I'd get bored."

Deborah Masson, Episode 142

"I'm a sketcher, I think. I'm definitely not a planner. I always have notebooks with me, thoughts going on in my head. I always have a pen to jot those down. And then I go back. I piece things together like a puzzle."

Shelley Read, Episode 184

"It's funny… when I started writing, I was very much a pantser. I would just plan a little bit, I'd have a notebook and fill it out with ideas and little titbits of my character's personality… what was driving them and things like that. I've evolved as a writer; I've gained an incredible appreciation for the importance of structure. I think a lot of pantsers probably actually follow structure, but they do so unconsciously."

Angela Ackerman, Episode 58

"I roughly plan the book chapter by chapter, very roughly. And then I write the beginning and end of the book, so I can see where it starts and where it ends and my character's personal journey. And then with each chapter, I'll do the dialogue or action first, whatever's driving that chapter forward."

Victoria Goldman, Episode 174

"I do find early is really good. First thing, there's that time before the world has woken up, or is just waking up. It's quite special. I won't look at emails, anything like that. And a couple of hours, or even an hour, at the start of the day, I find that I can write in a more lucid way without kind of having been bogged down by all the stuff that comes up in the course of a day."

Nick Hunt, Episode 195

"Even if it's just a five-minute writing exercise, I want to try and do that as often as I can just to keep my hand in the game."

Claire Handscombe, Episode 72

"One of the very important parts of my writing routine was my bath. I always had a bath at night and I used to write first thing in the morning. But the bath was so that I could lock the bathroom door and think, away from the kids. Then I could sleep on that. I would wake up to my early-morning writing time thinking, 'OK, now I know what I'm going to write.'"

Lizzie Enfield, Episode 134

"Joy is central to my writing process. I really prioritise preserving and cultivating joy, because I think it's such an uncertain thing to engage with. You don't know that you're going to finish a particular book, or that the book is going to resonate with the publisher. So the only thing I really have control over as a writer, is the writing. And I want to make that process as rewarding for myself as possible. I'm pushing myself to try and write that little bit better each time I sit down at my computer. It has to challenge and engage you, and it's about carving out that space for yourself."

Eliza Henry-Jones, Episode 194

"I think it's good to have a writing routine. I
do treat it like a job. I work from nine until
five, and then I log off, and I spend some time
with my wife. And maybe we'll be plotting
something at night, but I'm not usually
writing at night anymore. You have to find
the motivation that works for you. Like, if
people want to finish a book, and they want
it badly enough, they will, you know?"

Rebecca Thorne, Episode 252

"In the beginning, I tried to read too many books
and go to too many classes and take on board
too much advice, instead of just sitting down
and enjoying telling a story. You learn your own
process. I write a synopsis, a story outline really,
and then I need to get going. Then I'll do three
drafts before it goes to my editor. So you learn
your own pattern and get into your own rhythm."

Jo Thomas, Episode 140

"When I start to get an idea almost the
first thing I do is to write a blurb… it
starts me making decisions because when
you're faced with the blank page it can
feel overwhelming and you almost need to
start cutting down on possible choices."

Kate Harrison, Episode 123

"First drafts seem to take about a year and a half. I edit a bit as I go along, but about eighteen months from when I write the first words to when I write *the end*. Then maybe six months of editing, and that's really full-on eight-hour days, because I enjoy it so much. I find it quite hard to actually let it go and send it off."

Claire Fuller, Episode 67

"I like to sit and just get it all out of my head so that it's all on the page, even if it's absolute nonsense. I'll be writing a scene and I need to come up with a town and I'll just put loads of question marks in, or I'll write things in brackets to myself like, 'This is a terrible chapter, Neil, please make it better.' So then when I read it back, I laugh. I'd rather have 100,000 rubbish words than like five good words."

Neil J. Hart, Episode 231

On community

Writing is usually done alone, but it rarely survives that way. Somewhere along the line, most writers need other people, whether that's for encouragement, perspective, or an honest second pair of eyes. These reflections look at how support shows up, and how to use it without losing your own voice (or mind!).

"Author communities can be really useful, because it prepares you for critique."

Sarah Painter, Episode 94

"Make sure you have a team of ministering angels if you can, who are supporting you along the way, because the creative process can be very isolating. Whether it be through a formal writing group or friends who are willing to read your work, I think that that's been the most important thing. For me, the creative process is such a balance between isolation and concentration and community and sharing ideas, so I think that's been a really helpful thing through this process."

Bea Setton, Episode 173

"I suddenly had this group, and we were all talking about writing works in progress... and it just fitted naturally."

Roz Morris, Episode 106

"The other great thing that I got out of it is a writing community. Me and one other writer on this course, we formed a critique group. We've been meeting every month since then in a local pub and swapping whatever we're working on with each other."

Claire Fuller, Episode 67

"I brainstorm with friends and with my husband. I've got kind of a very small group of trusted brainstorming friends."

Tosca Lee, Episode 84

"I have my alpha and beta readers that I like to send it to. I've met quite a few lovely people on Twitter who I trust, and I can have these little conversations with and just say, what do you think to this, or do you think this works? They can read so much more into it than if I send it to family."

Gemma Denham, Episode 246

"Find other people who are coming out with debuts... just reach out to an author on social media."

Julia Kite, Episode 92

"My really conscientious teachers sent me
to the Suwannee Young Writers Conference,
which was this high school writing conference
for young writers… For the first time I was
in an environment that I was built for and
I was making friends with fellow weirdos
like me, who spent a lot of time alone,
writing about characters they'd made up."

Lillian Li, Episode 99

"Find your people is probably the best advice
and the best thing that I've done… I started
playing football with a group of guys I met on
Twitter, and a couple of them were writers. I'd
hear them swapping stories before the start,
and I just thought, these guys are just like me.
They've got jobs, they've got lives, and they're
writing on the side. Why can't I give it a go?"

Chris McDonald, Episode 233

On self-doubt, rejection and persistence

Doubt doesn't disappear once you start taking writing seriously. If anything, it gets louder. Rejection has a way of amplifying it, as well. These voices speak honestly about that cycle, and about the less glamorous but more important decision to keep going anyway.

"If anyone's listening to this, I genuinely mean it. Just have a go. What's the worst that can happen?"

Tony Schumacher, Episode 79

"Writing novels is terrifying... if I stopped and looked back, I think I would just think this is terrible and lose all confidence."

Will Dean, Episode 109

"You do have to look at your own work with a critical eye, but not too critical. You don't want to keep telling yourself that you're crap, but you have to know where your flaws are as a writer, and what you can improve on. Harlan Coben said a great thing – 'Only bad writers think they're good,' and he's probably right."

Steve Cavanagh, Episode 122

"I always told myself that the fault lay with
me and with the book and not necessarily
with the people I was sending it to."

Paul Howarth, Episode 79

"The rejections that I'd received on my
full manuscript... there were thirteen of
them... it's a business, it's not personal."

Sheena Kamal, Episode 83

"Rejection is part of a process. I published my first novel... after twelve drafts and giving up on it twice."

Michael Redhill, Episode 85

"The biggest hurdle is consistency, just
consistently being able to work. The way you
overcome that is persistence. It really is. And I tell
that to everybody. The only way you lose in this
thing, is if you quit. So just refuse to go away."

Matt Wallace, Episode 131

"Some days it's not about inspiration. It's just about doing it again."

Susanna Dickey, Episode 132

"As a stand-up comedian, I did an open spot competition. Afterwards, the organiser said, 'You're good, but don't apologise for being there.' And I think that's pretty much something you grow into. It's not always going to work, but just don't apologise, because you've got every right to be there."

Ian Moore, Episode 200

"It's persistence. You keep working the problem until it moves."

Bill Beverly, Episode 115

"Our ability as writers to see imperfection is a double-edged sword, you know? It is what drives us to create, but it can also become a burden along the way. You just have to be aware of that and allow yourself to, you know, create a shitty first draft."

Maram Taibah, Episode 127

"Rejection definitely made it better. I can write now as somebody with more life experience."

Sarah Painter, Episode 94

"Don't give up. The only difference between a published and unpublished writer is the refusal to take no for an answer and give up. So just keep going and if you're getting rejected, then that's just part of the process. Learn from that and keep writing."

Steph Broadribb, Episode 55

"Having worked in TV, it was a pretty good apprenticeship, because you have to be creative on demand and you learn the discipline of just doing something – which is 90% of the battle with writing. It doesn't matter how bad it is, because you can always improve it."

Simon Toyne, Episode 59

"Writing a novel, writing anything, is a marathon. It's a lot of commitment. It takes a lot of endurance. And there's a lot of self-doubt all the way through. You just have to be confident in your voice and trust yourself and keep going. I think what I've learned most as a writer is that you cannot beat yourself up if you don't get anything done for three days or three months. Sometimes if nothing comes, it's because it's for some reason, and you're refuelling. You're taking a break, but **you're not quitting.**"

Bonnie Garmus, Episode 168

14
Index of Contributors

The following is a list of the contributors quoted in this volume, with a short bio for each. Do take the time to look them up and read their work. A massive thanks to all of the guests I've interviewed over the years – without you, there would be no podcast.

Angela Ackerman (Chapters 6, 13)

Angela Ackerman is a writing coach and non-fiction author specialising in storytelling craft. She is best known as the co-creator of *The Emotion Thesaurus* series, a widely used set of reference books for writers. Through her books and teaching, she focuses on helping authors deepen characterisation, emotion and narrative impact.

Gail Aldwin (Chapters 1, 7, 13)

Gail Aldwin is a British novelist, poet and scriptwriter. She has been writing for over a decade. Her first two coming-of-age novels were runners-up in the Dorchester Literary Festival Writing Prize 2020 and 2022.

Tove Alsterdal (Chapter 3)

Tove Alsterdal is a Swedish crime novelist and journalist. Her novels include Women on the Beach and the High Coast series, including We Know You Remember (Swedish title: Rotvälta), which was awarded Best Swedish Crime Novel of the Year by the Swedish Crime Writers' Academy.

Rosanna Amaka (Chapters 5, 13)

Rosanna Amaka is a British novelist. Her debut novel, *The Book of Echoes*, was published by Doubleday and explores memory, community and the legacy of place. It was shortlisted for the Authors' Club Best First Novel Award, the RSL Christopher Bland Prize and the HWA Debut Crown Award.

Rachel Amphlett (Chapters 11, 13)

Rachel Amphlett is a British author writing crime and spy thrillers. She is best known for the *Kay Hunter* crime series and the *Dan Taylor* spy thriller novels. Her work is characterised by fast-paced plotting and a strong focus on investigative detail, and she also publishes independently.

Jessica Anthony (Chapter 13)

Jessica Anthony is an American novelist and short story writer. Her novels include *Enter the Aardvark, The Convalescent,* and *The Most,* which was longlisted for the National Book Award.

A.D. Barker (Chapter 13)

A.D. Barker is a British author writing dark, unsettling fiction. He is the author of the novel *Society Place* and several short story collections, with work that blends psychological horror, social unease and speculative elements.

Clare Beams (Chapter 13)

Clare Beams is the author of the story collection *We Show What We Have Learned*, which won the Bard Fiction Prize and was a Kirkus Best Debut of 2016, and the novel *The Illness Lesson*.

Bill Beverly (Chapter 13)

Bill Beverly is an American writer. His debut novel *Dodgers* won the Crime Writers' Association Gold Dagger. He is also the author of the novel *Sons of Ben* and the non-fiction book *On the Lam*.

D.V. Bishop (Chapter 8)

D.V. Bishop is a British author of historical crime fiction. He is best known for the *Cesare Aldo* series, which begins with *City of Vengeance* and is set in renaissance Florence. His novels combine meticulous historical research with fast-paced investigations and political intrigue.

Julia Boggio (Chapter 13)

Julia Boggio is a British novelist writing contemporary fiction. Her novels include *Shooters* and *Choke*, and more recently *Our Italian Summer*. Her work is character-driven and often explores relationships, ambition and the pressures people place on themselves and others.

Sarah Bonner (Chapters 8, 13)

Sarah Bonner is a British crime novelist. Her debut novel, *Her Perfect Twin*, is a psychological thriller exploring identity, obsession and the consequences of hidden pasts. She writes dark, contemporary crime fiction with a strong focus on character and moral tension.

Steph Broadribb (Chapter 13)

Steph Broadribb is a British crime novelist and former police officer. She is the author of the *Retired Detective Superintendent Alison McKenzie* series, which begins with *Deep Down Dead*.

Natasha Calder (Chapter 12)

Natasha Calder is a graduate of Clarion West 2018 and the author of *Whether Violent or Natural*, which was published in 2023 by Bloomsbury and The Overlook Press, and longlisted for the Nota Bene Prize 2024.

AJ Campbell (Chapter 2)

AJ Campbell is an Amazon USA top 40 bestselling author of twelve psychological suspense thrillers. She loves throwing characters into seemingly unbelievable situations and figuring it out from there. The result is thrillers full of twists, turns and torment, with gasp-worthy endings.

Edward Carey (Chapter 13)

Edward Carey is a British novelist and illustrator. He is the author of novels including *Observatory Mansions*, *Little* (a fictionalised portrait of Madame Tussaud) and *Edith Holler*.

Steve Cavanagh (Chapter 13)

Steve Cavanagh is a Northern Irish crime novelist and the author of the *Eddie Flynn* series, featuring a former con-man turned defence lawyer. His novels have won multiple crime fiction awards and have become international bestsellers. He is known for tightly plotted courtroom thrillers with high stakes and sharp twists.

Helen Cooper (Chapter 6)

Helen Cooper is a British author of psychological thrillers. Her novels include *The Downstairs Neighbour*, *The Other Guest*, *The Couple in the Photo* and *My Darling Boy*, which is set in a close-knit Derbyshire village.

Clio Cornish (Chapters 8, 13)

Clio Cornish is a British editor working primarily with fiction writers. She has edited across contemporary and literary fiction and is known for her focus on structure, clarity and character development. Alongside editorial work, she also writes fiction.

S.A. Cosby (Chapter 13)

S.A. Cosby is an American crime novelist writing gritty, socially engaged noir fiction. His novels include *Blacktop Wasteland* and *Razorblade Tears*, both of which received major critical acclaim and multiple awards.

Paddy Crewe (Chapter 13)

Paddy Crewe is an Irish novelist. His debut novel *My Name Is Yip* won the CWA John Creasey (New Blood) Dagger and was shortlisted for multiple crime fiction awards. He writes character-driven fiction that blends crime, humour, and social observation.

Liam J. Cross (Chapters 8, 13)

Liam J. Cross is a British screenwriter and script editor. He works across film and television, supporting story development, structure, and character at script stage. Alongside his screen work, he has spoken publicly about writing craft, collaboration and sustaining a professional writing career.

Leona Deakin (Chapter 13)

Leona Deakin is a psychologist and the author of four novels in the acclaimed *Dr Augusta Bloom* series: *Gone*, *Lost*, *Hunt*, and *The Imposter*. The series, published with Penguin Random House, has been a hit in the UK and across Europe.

Will Dean (Chapters 4, 6, 13)

Will Dean is a British crime novelist. He is best known for the *Tuva Moodyson* series, which begins with *Dark Pines* and is set in rural Sweden, as well as stand-alone thrillers including *The Last Thing to Burn*. His work is known for its strong sense of place, psychological tension and tightly plotted narratives.

Gemma Denham (Chapter 13)

Gemma Denham is a British author of crime and psychological fiction. She is the author of *The Storm*, a thriller centred on secrets, guilt and the consequences of past actions. Her work focuses on tension-driven storytelling and morally complex characters.

Susanna Dickey (Chapter 13)

Susanna Dickey is a Northern Irish novelist and short story writer. She is the author of *Common Decency*, which was shortlisted for the Waterstones Debut Fiction Prize and the Kate O'Brien Award. Her work is known for its sharp emotional insight, close attention to voice and exploration of intimacy, power and class.

Margaret Douaihy (Chapter 12)

Margaret Douaihy is an American crime novelist. She is the author of *Scorched Grace*, the first novel in the *Sister Holiday* series, featuring a punk, queer nun working as an amateur sleuth in New Orleans.

Rod Duncan (Chapter 13)

Rod Duncan is a British novelist writing speculative, historical and literary fiction. He is best known for *The Fall of the Gas-Lit Empire* series, a steampunk-influenced alternate history, and the standalone novel, *Dear Me*. His work often explores identity, history and the stories people tell themselves to survive.

Julian Dutton (Chapter 13)

Julian Dutton is a British writer and performer working across theatre, television and prose. He has a background in acting and creates character-led work that often draws on performance and voice. Alongside screen and stage projects, he also writes fiction.

Clare Empson (Chapter 10)

Clare Empson is a British thriller writer. Her debut novel *Him* is a psychological thriller centred on obsession and coercive control. She writes dark, tension-driven fiction focused on power dynamics and emotional manipulation.

Lizzie Enfield (Chapter 13)

Lizzie Enfield is a journalist and regular contributor to national newspapers, magazines and radio. She has written five novels, one non-fiction title and had short stories broadcast on Radio Four and published in various magazines and anthologies.

Christopher Fowler (Chapter 13)

Christopher Fowler was the multi award-winning author of forty-five novels and short story collections, and the author of the *Bryant & May* mysteries. His novels include *Roofworld, Spanky, Psychoville, Calabash* and the award-winning *Paperboy* and *Film Freak*.

Claire Fuller (Chapter 13)

Claire Fuller is a British novelist writing literary and contemporary fiction. Her novels include *Our Endless Numbered Days, Swimming Lessons* and *Unsettled Ground*, which won the Costa Novel Award. Her work is known for its psychological depth, unreliable narration and exploration of family, memory and survival.

Bonnie Garmus (Chapters 12, 13)

Bonnie Garmus is an American novelist best known for her debut novel *Lessons in Chemistry*. The book became an international bestseller and was adapted into a television series. Before turning to fiction, she worked as a copywriter and creative director, bringing a sharp, observational voice to her writing.

Victoria Goldman (Chapter 13)

Victoria Goldman is a novelist, freelance journalist, editor and proofreader. Her debut crime novel, *The Redeemer*, was shortlisted for Best Debut Crime Novel of 2022 in the Crime Fiction Lover Awards 2022. The sequel, *The Associate*, was the Editor's Choice Winner of Best Indie Crime Novel of 2023 in the Crime Fiction Lover Awards 2023.

Claire Handscombe (Chapter 13)

Claire Handscombe is the author of *Unscripted*, a novel about a young woman with a celebrity crush and a determined plan, and the editor of *Walk With Us: How The West Wing Changed Our Lives*. She also hosts *The Brit Lit Podcast*, a fortnightly show of news and views from British books and publishing.

Neil J. Hart (Chapter 13)

Neil J Hart is a British author of teen and YA fiction, writing fantasy, sci-fi and horror adventure. His books include *The Last Scarecrow* and *Sadie Madison and the Boy in the Crimson Scarf*, and he also writes the *Harper Hale* sci-fi adventure series.

Joey Hartstone (Chapter 13)

Joey Hartstone is an American novelist and screenwriter. He is the author of the legal thriller *The Local*, and has also worked extensively in television as a writer and producer, including on Marvel's *Luke Cage* and *Agents of S.H.I.E.L.D.*

Emily Houghton (Introduction)

Emily Houghton is a British novelist writing contemporary and romantic fiction. Her debut novel, *Before I Saw You*, was published in 2020 and explores relationships, missed connections, and emotional vulnerability.

Dan Howarth (Chapters 6, 12)

Dan Howarth is a writer from the North of England. He's the author of dark, powerful fiction including *Last Night of Freedom, Lionhearts* and *Territory*. His work has been published both in print and online, most notably at *The Other Stories* podcast, where his stories have been downloaded over 100,000 times.

Paul Howarth (Chapter 13)

Paul Howarth is a British-Australian novelist and former lawyer. His debut novel, *Only Killers and Thieves*, was published in 2018 and won the Barnes & Noble Discover Award for best fiction. He is also the author of *Dust Off the Bones*, an historical thriller.

Nick Hunt (Chapter 13)

Nick Hunt has walked and written across much of Europe. His articles have appeared in *The Economist, The Guardian* and other publications, and he works as an editor for the

Dark Mountain Project. His first book, *Walking the Woods and the Water*, was a finalist for the Stanford Dolman Travel Book of the Year.

Hanna Jameson (Chapters 1, 13)

Hanna Jameson is a British novelist writing speculative and contemporary fiction. She is the author of *The Last*, a climate-driven thriller set in a Swiss hotel at the end of the world, and *Old Sins*, a literary crime novel.

Matt Johnson (Chapter 10)

Matt Johnson is a British crime thriller author and former soldier/Metropolitan Police officer, best known for his *Wicked Game* trilogy and *Crow 27*. Drawing from 25 years of policing experience, his novels are characterised by high-octane, realistic portrayals of terrorism and crime.

Milly Johnson (Chapter 4)

Milly Johnson is the author of novels, short story e-books, poetry and a Quick Reads Novella (*The Little Dreams of Lara Cliffe*) and was an erstwhile leading copywriter for the greetings card industry. She is also a newspaper columnist and a seasoned after-dinner speaker.

Eliza Henry-Jones (Chapter 13)

Eliza Henry-Jones is an author based in the Yarra Valley of Victoria, Australia. Her novels have been listed for awards including the Readings Prize for New Australian Fiction, QLD Literary Awards, NSW Premier's Literary Awards, Indie Awards, ABIA Awards and CBCA Awards.

Jackie Kabler (Chapter 13)

Jackie Kabler is a television presenter and award-winning crime writer. Her bestselling psychological thrillers have sold over a million copies in English alone and have been translated into nine other languages. They include *Am I Guilty?*, *The Perfect Couple* and *The Vanishing of Class 3B*.

Sheena Kamal (Chapter 13)

Sheena Kamal is a Canadian crime novelist. She is best known for the *Nora Watts* series, beginning with *The Lost Ones*, which features a tough, unconventional private investigator. Her work blends noir sensibilities with explorations of identity, family and survival.

Lesley Kara (Chapters 3, 13)

Lesley Kara is the Sunday Times bestselling author of multiple psychological thrillers including The Rumour, Who Did You Tell?, The Other Tenant and her latest novel Troublemaker. Her debut, The Rumour, was a breakout success and has since been adapted for television.

Ruth Kelly (Chapter 8)

Ruth Kelly is an award-winning journalist who has ghosted a string of Sunday Times top-ten bestsellers – most recently *The Prison Doctor*, which sold over 250,000 copies, and *The Governor*, which went straight in at number one on the Amazon charts and number five in the Sunday Times bestseller list.

Julia Kite (Chapter 9)

Julia Kite describes herself as a New Yorker and ex-Londoner who can't quit writing. She's insatiably curious, eager to learn and passionate about writing. Her debut novel, *The Hope and Anchor*, was published in February 2018.

Zoe Lea (Chapter 7)

Zoe Lea is a British author renowned for her psychological thrillers that delve into complex human relationships and suspenseful narratives. She lives in the Lake District with her family and has had all kinds of career roles including being a teacher, photographer and freelance journalist.

Tosca Lee (Chapters 9, 13)

Tosca Lee is a New York Times bestselling author of twelve novels including *The Line Between*, *The Progeny*, *The Legend of Sheba*, *Iscariot* and *The Long March Home*. Her work has been translated into seventeen languages and optioned for TV and film.

Lillian Li (Chapter 3)

Lillian Li is the author of the novel *Number One Chinese Restaurant*, which was an NPR Best Book of 2018, and longlisted for the Women's Prize and the Center for Fiction's First Novel Prize. Her work has been published in *The New York Times*, *Granta*, *One Story*, *bon appétit*, *Travel & Leisure*, *The Guardian* and *Jezebel*.

Sarah Leipciger (Chapter 9)

Sarah Leipciger lives in London with her three children. She is an Associate Lecturer in Creative Writing at Birkbeck, University of London and also teaches at City Lit, London. Her short fiction has been shortlisted for the Asham Award, the Fish Prize and the Bridport Prize. She is the author of the critically acclaimed *The Mountain Can Wait*, *Coming Up for Air* and *Moon Road*.

Charlotte Levin, (Chapter 2)

Charlotte Levin is the bestselling author of *If I Can't Have You* and Richard & Judy Book Club pick, *If I Let You Go*. She has been shortlisted for the Andrea Badenoch Award, part of the New Writers North Awards, and has written for publications, including *The Observer* and *Marie Claire*.

John Lincoln (Chapter 5)

John Lincoln is the transparent pseudonym of John Williams, the novelist, biographer and crime fiction reviewer for *The Mail on Sunday*. His first book, *Into the Badlands*, has become a crime fiction classic. His true crime account of a notorious miscarriage of justice, *Bloody Valentine*, is a cult classic, described by Benjamin Zephaniah as his favourite book.

Sean Lusk (Chapter 13)

Sean Lusk is a novelist. His debut, *The Second Sight of Zachary Cloudesley*, was a BBC2 *Between the Covers* pick, a Sunday Times Historical Fiction Book of the Month, and longlisted for the Walter Scott Prize and the Goldsboro Books Glass Bell Award.

Bonnie MacBird (Chapter 8)

Bonnie MacBird is an American novelist and screenwriter best known for her *Sherlock Holmes Adventures* series, which continues the Conan Doyle canon. Her novels include *Art in the Blood*, *Unquiet Spirits* and *The Devil's Due*. She has also worked extensively in film and television, with writing credits including *Tron* and *The Twilight Zone*.

Melanie McGrath (Chapter 13)

Melanie McGrath is an award-winning writer of bestselling fiction and nonfiction. As MJ McGrath she is the author of the acclaimed Edie Kiglatuk series of Arctic mysteries, twice longlisted for the CWA Gold Dagger and picked as Times and Financial Times thrillers of the year.

Juman Malouf (Chapter 13)

Juman Malouf was born in Beirut, Lebanon and grew up in London. She graduated from Brown University with a BA in Fine Arts and Art History. She has designed and illustrated for theatre, film and fashion in the US and Europe. *The Trilogy of Two* was her first novel.

Deborah Masson (Chapter 13)

Deborah Masson is a British crime novelist. She is the author of the *DI Eve Hunter* series, which is set in Edinburgh and blends police procedural investigation with psychological depth. Her work focuses on complex cases, moral ambiguity and the personal cost of policing.

Chris McDonald (Chapter 13)

Chris McDonald is the author the *Erika Piper* series, the *Stonebridge Mysteries* and *Little Ghost*. Under his pen name, Chris Frost, he's the author of the festive bestselling crime book, *The Killer's Christmas List*.

Madeleine Milburn (Chapter 9)

Madeleine Milburn is on the committee of the Association of Authors' Agents (AAA) and has appeared on The Bookseller's list of the 150 most influential people in the book trade every year since 2017. Madeleine was awarded Literary Agent of the Year at the British Book Awards in 2018.

Stefan Mohamed (Chapters 11, 13)

Stefan Mohamed is a British novelist writing fiction for adults and young readers. He is the author of *The House on Utopia Way*, a contemporary novel exploring masculinity, friendship and personal reinvention, as well as earlier works including *Bitter Sixteen*. His writing often examines identity, social pressure and the tension between aspiration and reality.

Ian Moore (Chapter 13)

Ian Moore is a British author and comedian writing comic crime fiction. He is best known for the *Death and Croissants* series, which begins with the titular novel, blending murder mystery with humour and expat life in rural France.

Nikki Moore (Chapter 7)

Nikki Moore is the author of the popular *#LoveLondon* series, attracting four- and five-star reviews on Amazon. A number of her novellas featured in the top 100 short story charts on Kobo and the top 20 in the Amazon UK Bestsellers Holiday chart.

Roz Morris (Chapter 13)

Roz Morris is a British author, editor and writing coach. She writes fiction and non-fiction, including the novel *Not Quite Lost* and the craft book *Nail Your Novel*. She is known for her work on narrative structure, revision and helping writers develop clarity and momentum in their storytelling.

Lauren North (Chapters 1, 9)

Lauren North is a British author of psychological thrillers. Her novels include *One Step Behind*, *The Perfect Son*, and *Safe at Home*. She also writes book club thrillers as LC North and steamy sports romances as Bella North.

Angela C Nurse (Chapter 11)

Angela C Nurse was born in the Kingdom of Fife. She spent her teenage years in Penzance before returning to Scotland. Her *Rowan McFarlane Mysteries* are set within the fictional town of Cuddieford, which lies somewhere between Dunfermline and Kirkcaldy.

Merle Nyegate (Chapters 4, 5, 13)

Merle Nyegate is a British writer working in espionage fiction and television drama. She writes spy and thriller stories alongside working as a TV script editor, where she develops and refines scripts for broadcast. Her work spans prose and screen, with a strong focus on tension, character and narrative structure.

Nathan O'Hagan (Chapter 7)

Nathan O'Hagan is a British writer and co-founder of Obliterati Press. His debut novel, *The World Is (Not) A Cold*

Dead Place was published by Armley Press in 2015. He has also written about politics, culture, football, and men's mental health and wellbeing for *Byline Times*, *The New European*, *Men's Fitness*, *FourFourTwo*, *Metro*, *Morningstar*, *Sabotage Times* and *Clash Music*.

Sarah Painter (Chapters 2, 13)

Sarah Painter is a British novelist writing urban fantasy and contemporary fiction. Her books include *In the Light of What We See*, *The Language of Spells* and the *Crow Investigations* series. She is known for blending everyday settings with magical elements and for character-driven storytelling.

Elena Passarello (Chapter 13)

Elena Passarello is an American essayist and non-fiction author. She is the author of *Animals Strike Curious Poses*, a collection exploring the relationships between humans, animals and culture, and *Let Me Clear My Throat*.

Laura Pearson (Chapters 6, 12)

Laura Pearson is a British author writing contemporary and book club fiction. Her novels include *The Last List of Mabel Beaumont*, *I Wanted You to Know* and *Nobody's Wife*. She is known for emotionally driven stories that focus on relationships, memory and resilience.

Joanna Penn (Chapters 4, 11, 13)

Joanna Penn is a British author of fiction and non-fiction and the host of *The Creative Penn Podcast*. She writes thrillers and speculative fiction, including the *ARKANE* series, alongside books for writers on creativity, publishing and the author business.

Shelley Read (Chapter 13)

Shelley Read is a fifth generation Coloradoan who lives with her family in the Elk Mountains of the Western Slope. She has written for *The Denver Post* and a variety of publications. *Go as a River*, her first novel, was published in over twenty-five territories.

Michael Redhill (Chapter 13)

Michael Redhill is a Canadian novelist, poet and essayist. He is the author of *Bellevue Square*, which won the Scotiabank Giller Prize 2017, along with other novels including *Martin Sloane* and *Consolation*.

Scott Reintgen (Chapter 7)

Scott Reintgen is the NYT bestselling author of *A Door in the Dark*. He also wrote the *Nyxia* series, *The Problem with Prophecies* and the *Ashlords* duology. He's a former public school teacher from North Carolina.

Senta Rich (Chapter 13)

Senta Rich began her career as an advertising copywriter. During this time, she also wrote radio plays and magazine articles, before moving into the world of screenwriting. She now writes regularly for film and TV.

Bead Roberts (Chapters 2, 13)

Bead Roberts is a writer and writing tutor, twice nominated for the Writing Tutor of The Year awards. She has written plays and stories for radio and had more than a hundred of her stories published in women's magazines.

Becky Robison (Chapter 13)

Becky Robison is a writer living in Louisville, Kentucky. A graduate of UNLV's Creative Writing MFA program, her work has appeared in *Salon*, *Slate*, *Business Insider*, and elsewhere.

Mac Rogers (Chapter 13)

Mac Rogers is an award-winning playwright based in New York City. His plays have earned acclaim from *The New York Times*, *Backstage*, *The Wall Street Journal*, *Time Out New York*, *New York Post* and many others.

Karin Salvalaggio (Chapters 2, 13)

Karin Salvalaggio is an American crime novelist. She is best known for the *Detective Colleen Cruz* series, which begins with *Bone Dust White* and is set in Montana.

Tony Schumacher (Chapters 1, 6, 13)

Tony Schumacher is an English novelist and scriptwriter from Liverpool, best known for his *John Rossett* alternate-history thriller series, which begins with *The Darkest Hour* and continues with *The British Lion*. He previously worked as a police officer and wrote the BBC drama, *Responder*.

Melissa Sercia (Chapter 11)

Melissa Sercia is an award-winning urban fantasy and paranormal romance author with a passion for philosophy, mythology and all things supernatural. She is the author of the *Blood and Darkness* series, *Beautiful Dark Beasts* series and *Immortal Billionaires* series.

Bea Setton (Chapter 13)

Bea Setton is a British novelist writing contemporary and literary fiction. Her debut novel, *Berlin*, explores grief, friendship and identity through the story of a woman navigating life in the German capital.

William Shaw (Chapters 6, 13)

William Shaw is a British crime novelist and journalist. He is best known for the *Alex Cupidi* series, set in Kent, and his *Breen & Tozer* books. His work often blends meticulous research with character-driven investigations and a strong sense of place.

Mark Stevens (Chapter 5)

Mark Stevens has worked as a reporter, television news producer and in public relations. He's the author of *The Fireballer* and *The Allison Coil Mystery* series, including *Antler Dust* and *The Melancholy Howl*.

Jo Thomas (Chapter 13)

Jo Thomas is a British bestselling author of romantic fiction. She is known for novels such as *The Olive Branch*, *The Oyster Catcher* and *Escape to the French Farmhouse*, which often combine romance with food, travel and a strong sense of place. Her books regularly appear in the UK bestseller charts.

Rebecca Thorne (Chapters 3, 11, 13)

Rebecca Thorne is a USA Today, Indie, and Sunday Times bestselling author, specializing in fantasy, sci-fi and romance. She is a proud member of the LGBTQIA+ community, lives near Denver, Colorado, and uses her ADHD as a superpower to write multiple books a year.

Maram Taibah (Chapters 1, 13)

Maram Taibah is a Saudi children's fantasy author, screenwriter and film director. As an author, she has self-published a steampunk fantasy novella for middle-grade readers, the first in the *Cerulean Universe* Series.

Simon Toyne (Chapter 13)

Simon Toyne is a British thriller novelist and former television journalist and producer. He is the author of the *Sanctus* trilogy, beginning with *Sanctus*, which blends religious history with high-concept suspense.

C.J. Tudor (Chapters 12, 13)

C.J. Tudor is a British author of thriller and speculative fiction. She is best known for her debut novel *The Chalk Man*, which became an international bestseller, as well as subsequent novels including *The Taking of Annie Thorne* and *The Burning Girls*. Her work is known for blending suspense, psychological tension and darker speculative elements.

Emma Viskic (Chapter 13)

Emma Viskic wrote the critically acclaimed *Caleb Zelic* series, which has been published worldwide. *Resurrection Bay* won the Ned Kelly Award for Best First Fiction and an unprecedented three Davitt Awards.

Joanna Wallace (Chapter 1)

Joanna Wallace is a British author whose debut novel *You'd Look Better as a Ghost* won Best Debut Crime Novel of the year in the Crime Fiction Lover Awards, with Joanna also being shortlisted for Best Crime Author. Her second novel, *The Dead Friend Project,* was published by Viper in July 2024 and was a Literary Review crime novel of the year.

Matt Wallace (Chapter 13)

Matt Wallace is the Hugo Award-winning author of *Rencor: Life in Grudge City*, the *Sin du Jour* series and *Savage Legion*. He's also penned over 100 short stories in addition to writing for film and television.

Ericka Waller (Chapters 1, 10)

Ericka Waller is a British novelist writing contemporary fiction. Her novels include *Dog Days*, *A Girl Like You* and *Love, Unscripted*. Her work often explores themes of grief, connection and resilience, with a strong focus on character and emotional honesty.

Louise Walters (Chapter 13)

Louise Walters is a British writer, editor and publisher. She is the founder of the independent press, Louise Walters Books, which focuses on distinctive literary fiction and underrepresented voices.

David Wappel (Chapter 13)

David Wappel is an American screenwriter working in film and television. He has written for a range of studio and independent projects, often focusing on character-driven stories within genre frameworks. Alongside screen work, he has discussed craft, discipline and the realities of a professional writing career.

S.J. Watson (Chapter 13)

S.J. Watson is a British author best known for the psychological thriller *Before I Go to Sleep*, which became an international bestseller and was adapted into a feature film. His subsequent novels include *Second Life* and *Final Cut*.

CJ Walley (Chapter 10)

CJ Walley is a spec scriptwriter from Staffordshire, England. His scripts have been featured by Amazon Studios and he recently penned the LA-based feature films *Break Even*, *Double Threat* and *Night Train*. He is also the author of screenwriting book *Turn and Burn*.

Acknowledgments

Firstly, I want to thank every single one of the guests I've had the privilege to chat to since I began the show in 2014. If your quote didn't make it into this volume, it's no reflection on you, or your ability to drop pearls of wisdom. It was a mammoth task to try to wrangle hundreds of hours of audio transcripts, let alone choose which comments to include, so please don't take it personally. There will be more *Write Here, Write Now* volumes in the future so, chances are, you'll pop up in one of those.

A special handful of those guests actually helped me to refine the book, by agreeing to read early drafts and give me their feedback. Thanks go to Dan Howarth, Lauren North and Gemma Denham, for their invaluable advice.

I'm grateful to my copy editor, Debra Newhouse – a patient and precise expert in her field and always a pleasure to work with. Any minor errors you have found in the book are almost certainly mine.

A huge thanks to John Williams, my high school English teacher, who encouraged, challenged and never patronised me. He was the first person outside of my family to make me believe I could be a writer.

I'll give Lauren North another mention, along with

Bead Roberts, for being excellent mentors and helping to shape not only my writing, but my attitude towards it. The truth is, almost all of the writers I've met, interviewed, collaborated with, taught or mentored have fuelled my passion for the craft and confirm what I've known for a long time: we are all in it together… so don't even think about giving up!

Happy writing, stay safe, and I'll see you next time.

About the author

Wayne Kelly is an author, writing coach and mentor. He is passionate about helping and inspiring other writers and produces educational courses and content. He helps other authors release their books with his imprint, Pick Lock Publishing. Take a look at wkwproductions.co.uk/selfpublishing for more information.

He is the producer of the award-winning feature length documentary, NO FARE: The Sian Green Story. In addition to his crime novels, Safe Hands and The Call Back, he's written and directed several short films including IN-KLING, which was an official selection at the International HorrorHound Film Festival in Ohio. Since 2014 he's hosted The Write Place podcast (formerly known as The Joined Up Writing Podcast), where he interviews successful authors about their books, writing and journeys to publication. With his limited spare time, he's a singer-songwriter with The Wry Dogs and devoted dad to Meg and cat father to Milo. He loves to cycle around the beautiful Leicestershire countryside, where he lives with his long-suffering wife, Alyson. To find out more and to download your free Writer's Survival Kit and Real Writers Never Quit poster, go to realwritersneverquit.com

Finally, please take a moment to leave a rating and review for this book. It really does help new authors reach a wider audience.